CALLED TO BE A LAYMAN

CALLED TO BE A LAYMAN

Gus Gustafson

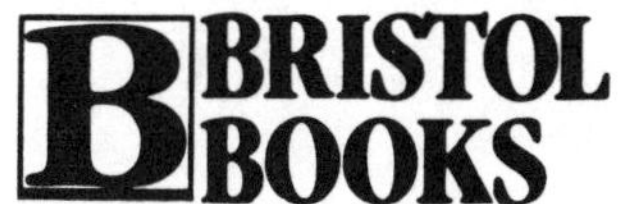

Called To Be A Layman

Published by Bristol Books

Revised Edition, 1989
Second Printing, March 1992
Third Printing, June 1993
Fourth Printing, July 1994
Fifth Printing, December 1994
Sixth Printing, October 1995
Seventh Printing, August, 1996
Eighth Printing, August 1998

This book was previously published as *I Was... Called to be a Layman,* copyright 1982 © by Abingdon Press.

Library of Congress Card Number: 89-61586
ISBN: 0-917851-36-6

Suggested Subject Headings:
1. Christian Life—Methodist Authors
2. Laity
Recommended Dewey Decimal Classification: 262'.15

Bristol Books
An imprint of Bristol House, Ltd.
P.O. Box 4020
Anderson, IN 46013
Phone: 765 644-0856 Fax: 765 622-1045
To order, call toll free 1-800-451-READ (7323)

To my mother and father, Esther and Joseph Gustafson, who, as I rebelled against godly teaching and a Christian home, prayed far into the nights, loved, disciplined, forgave, and got me to the Gust F. Johnson revival meeting.

To our extended family and the Monroe Evangelical Free Church, who encouraged me in my bitter, youthful disappointment of not being able to be a preacher and thus prepared me for God's special call.

To my wife, Estelle, who understood my call, bet her life on it, and became a wonderful, loving partner in fulfilling it.

CONTENTS

FOREWORD

I am fortunate to be the bishop in the area where Gus Gustafson serves as a lay leader. As a person, he is outstanding in every way and gives conference- and area-wide leadership. He is also a devout, hard-working member of his local church, First United Methodist Church in Griffin, Georgia.

However, until I read his manuscript *"I was . . . called to be a layman"* I did not realize his literary talents. I know that he is a committed Christian and that the radiance of his life shines in all he does. And he has been able to transcribe all this into print.

This book is an exciting and dynamic account that is largely personal. At the same time, he draws on the experiences of others, persons whom he knows and who form a part of his wider experience.

The arrangement of the book is inspirational, as well as logical. He appropriately begins with God's call. He then shows us how we should respond and outlines the need for an immediate response to divine grace. If we make this response, then God prepares us, and we are enabled to serve, first within our own family unit and then locally and throughout the world.

The Wesleyan note shines brightly in the third section of the book, which is entitled "God Empowers." Every hour of every day should be devoted to God's service. This does not mean that we should neglect our profession. But whatever our work, or profession may be, we belong to God, and our personal lives, possessions, and vocations are subject to his will and disposition. If we realize this, we know that we were born to win, not just for ourselves, but for God. We are at our best when we relax in his omnipotent will. Then, the power to answer the call is ours. That call is the high calling of God in Christ Jesus.

"I was . . . called to be a layman" is a marvelous book. I commend it highly. It is a testimony, and, at the same time, it is a guide book. It tells us how we can make our own testimony, recognizing that each is unique because every individual is unique. God does not duplicate in his creation. Each of us is distinctly himself or herself, with something to offer that no one else has.

William R. Cannon
Bishop, Raleigh Area
The United Methodist Church

ACKNOWLEDGMENTS

The various chapter titles represent the unfolding emphasis of God's call to me.

My thrilling discovery, as I pulled together information, was that some of my friends had encounters that were more vivid and dramatic than mine. They were willing to share these with me. So, with divine leading and their generosity, we have an inspiring compendium of adventures resulting from Christ's call to different laypeople to serve him, in various ways, in several different denominations, and from the stance of many vocational responsibilities.

Several close friends expressed special interest in the nature of this book. They took time out of their very busy lives to act as my advisors, critics, and sounding boards, chapter by chapter, as I listened to translate the Lord's word to me onto paper. These gracious people are Bill Knight, editor of *Griffin Daily News;* our son Gerrit, pastor of Gulf Coast Covenant Church; Merrill Arnold, author and senior partner of the Arnold Company, specialists in personnel development; Jim Snead, director of United Methodist Men, Board of Discipleship, The United Methodist Church.

Finally, the alpha and omega of this work is my dear wife and most constructive critic, Estelle, who reviewed, typed, retyped, and put the manuscript in good form from the first word to the last, so it could be more easily read and understood.

These people and many others have been inspired helpers in sharing the good news of Jesus Christ for all kinds of living.

PREVIEW

In comparison with others, I see myself as another very ordinary guy—struggling to make a decent living for a family, keeping my head above water, trying to make marks in a vocation, enjoying and rearing my children in a respectable manner. Through it all, there is the search for an honest-to-goodness, and a motivating, purpose for living (reality, some people call it).

But when I think of life with my Creator, I do not feel ordinary. A feeling surfaces of excitement and charmed living. It is hard to describe and probably harder to understand, unless you have been there. I see the times when the Lord of life multiplies my efforts and leads in a special, preferential way, as though I am one of his favorites. Something tells me: This is it. I have found it.

My double vision is probably very much like the picture each committed Christian has of himself or herself. Responding to God's call for commitment started the charmed part of my life. This led to my vocational call, which is the point of this book.

God calls us all, laity as well as clergy, to specific tasks.

Elton Trueblood says, "It is just as important for one boy to decide to be a Christian businessman as it is for another boy to decide to become a Christian clergyman."[1] If either one or both of these decisions are based on a personal call from God, it will begin a life of great fulfillment, of notable service to humanity, and of the miraculous leading and the exciting, everyday presence of the divine Holy Spirit.

My thesis emerges: God has a special, individual call for every Christ-committed layperson.

To this thought let us add the idea: the effectiveness of Christianity in our world today depends a great deal on the degree to which the great body of laypeople recognize and respond to God's call for their individual lives. The fate of our nation, many maintain, is related to the impact of Christianity on our culture. Therefore, as Christian laity, we see the awesome responsibility and the enormous opportunity of heeding and responding to God's call with the words of the prophet, "'Here am I! Send me'" (Isaiah 6:8*b*).

This book shares life experiences—mine and several friends'—in answering God's call to us. Response to that call gives our lives an element of great ongoing adventure, full of dangers and discoveries. We have uncovered a thrilling purpose for our being. It is as though, somehow, we have fallen heir to the motivating experience of being anointed for special living. What a thrilling way to live.

Beginning a venture always takes initiative, courage, and wisdom. This is especially true in the great experiment we are contemplating. Actually, it is a commitment—to try out the Almighty. It is sacred—no ordinary trial run. It is the greatest response we can ever make with our lives.

That is my discovery, and this book shares experiences that lead to light and to validate the venture. As we relate in our common quest, hear the "still small voice" (1 Kings 19:12*b*), and respond by risking our lives, life becomes exciting and meaningful.

So let us join in the search. Our Creator stands ready to guide our quests into something deeply satisfying and wonderful for ourselves—and others.

EXPERIENCE I

God Calls

When we commit our lives to Jesus Christ, many radical changes take place, many new opportunities come our way. One of the most exciting is his call to purposeful living.

Often, we take this call for granted, even ignore it, going on with life as usual. But to do so is to miss out on the riches of kingdom living.

In contrast to life as usual, Christ's urgent call is to a special assignment in kingdom building for each one of us. We are the elect for that unique place in life. More than any other group, laypeople are needed by God to advance his interests in fashioning the future of the world. For those of us who are ready to hear and are quick to respond, rewards are great and assured.

CHAPTER 1

Called . . .

*"You will be told what you must do." (Acts 9:6*b, *GNB)*

Frustrated and angry after struggling for months, I was waiting and ready to fight it out with God.

We had just finished stacking hay on the Jones 80 (acres) about two miles from home. The loose bunches had been pitched into the rack, now a full load.

"Milton," said my father, "you take the team—Molly and Flory—and the hayrack home. Wes and I will go in the car."

Here's my chance, I thought. *We'll go to the mat and find out where I stand.* These and other thoughts indignantly flashed through my mind. The ongoing battle had come into sharp focus: I wanted to be a preacher; God was not opening doors.

It started with my miraculous conversion, that fall when a high school junior. My teen-age rebellion against the disciplines of a godly, Christian home was well-known throughout our community. The resultant habits and activities were leading me into deeper and deeper trouble. Watching me develop, neighbors shook their heads. My family prayed.

Then, Gust F. Johnson, a Swedish evangelist, came to Aurora, Nebraska. My parents somehow got me to the meetings. This small town revival turned out to be my Damascus Road experience.

My Damascus Road

Along with six other young fellows in the far back southeast corner of the Christian church, I was cutting up. It was upsetting the people in that packed sanctuary, including the preacher.

Like a bolt of lightning, suddenly hitting, came the words of the Reverend Johnson, as he pointed a finger directly at us, "Young men, in the name of Almighty God, I command you, listen to what he has to say tonight. And do it while you can. This could be your last chance."

Struck with this fiery pronouncement, the fear of the Lord hung over us. We came to attention and listened, especially me. Under the spell of the eloquent, God-proclaiming Swede, guilt, remorse, and fear swept through my being. But Gust F. held out the hope and love of Jesus Christ.

The invitation was given. As the choir led the congregational singing, I broke, hearing the words.

> Just as I am, though tossed about
> With many a conflict, many a doubt,
> Fightings and fears within, without,
> O Lamb of God, I come, I come!

Pushing over the knees of the fellows and out of the pew, I headed down that long aisle toward the altar.

Emotions engulfed me. The sense of anyone being around was gone. It seemed like I was absolutely alone except that some irresistible power was pulling me to the altar and to my knees. My body was trembling and my heart pleading that God would forgive my sins.

As I again became conscious of people around me and my eyes opened, my parents and the preacher, Peter Olson, came into focus. They gave assurance of love, spoke words of hope from the Bible, and thanked God for what he was doing.

That night, my life's direction was turned around. I was converted—a new person—born again. The apostle Paul's words described me. "For if a man is in Christ he becomes a new person altogether—the past is finished and gone, everything has become fresh and new" (2 Corinthians 5:17, Phillips).

I had repented. God and my family forgave me. I could feel it, and I accepted it. With the love, understanding, support, and courageous integrity of my father, we went to businesses and people and made restitution for thievery and other wrongs I had done. They all forgave me.

What freedom, even for a fifteen-year-old. My entire being soared. I wanted to tell others—far and wide—about the redeeming power and joy of Jesus Christ. What was the quickest way? My answer: Be a preacher. God had different ideas.

Say Something, God

It was the time of the Great Depression, which began with the crash of '29. Hogs grown for family butchering were often sold, as a desperate effort to get a little urgently needed cash, leaving no meat for our table. The Great Plains drought had begun, finally resulting in the Dust Bowl. Farmers raked up tumbleweeds (Russian thistles) to feed cattle.

There seemed to be no way to start preparation for preaching. I was upset and disillusioned.

With new goals and difficult circumstances in my life, I got into the hayrack and headed the trusty, beautiful team of bay mares toward home. They knew the way and which side of the road to follow. The reins hung on the stick in front of the rack, while I stretched out in the hay, looked heavenward, and started quizzing God.

I could not stand the hopeless, dark hours any longer. These months of struggle in the Slough of Despond prompted the ultimatum: *God, either get me going, or you go your way and I'll go mine.*

Questions raced through my mind. *If you're so mighty, who don't you let me go? Are you able? Have I misunderstood you? Don't I have faith? What's wrong? I'm willing, why aren't you? Am I really saved?*

I don't remember the whole dialogue. It was mostly

one-way talk, from me. But I do remember the place. It happened at the second mud puddle after turning off the road, while going down that two-hundred-yard-long, tree-lined lane toward home.

At the muddy dip, I heard this answer to my questions: "Milton, I want you to serve me in everyday life, where the temptations are the toughest."

To my young heart, the meaning of those words was *"Trust me. I've got a place for you. Go on and finish high school here at home, Aurora. Be my witness where you are."*

Some time after hearing that voice, the meaning became clear:

God Called Me to Be a Layman

Even now, when recalling the experience, my heart beats faster, and tears come. Those words are the North Star of my life.

I try to thank God for speaking at that time, but no expression seems to suffice. So, I thank him and try to be his man where he places me and to do what he wills.

Reflecting now in a fast, panoramic view from that day to this, there emerge the uncharted paths, unexpected turns in the road, testings, victories, uncertainties, joys, challenges, seeming defeats, and excitement to which this call has led. Clearly, as he gave me the call, he also offered his hand. He led then and continues to lead now.

Sometimes I have wondered: *Was my call a response to the winds or pressures of the day, rather than to God's long-term purpose for my life?* It could be, but it is hard to believe from what followed.

Shortly after accepting the Lord's words, I was awarded a 4-H Club scholarship by the Union Pacific Railroad to attend the University of Nebraska, College of Agriculture. This was the first of a series of events leading me through the university without any money from home.

The Lord could have just as easily provided money for

attending the Bible academy. Instead, he used circumstances to close that door. In turn, doors opened that fulfilled his call to me.

This was a discovery early in my Christian pilgrimage—when God closes doors, he opens others, which bring fulfillment and excitement beyond imagination or dreams. "No mere man has ever seen, heard or even imagined what wonderful things God has ready for those who love the Lord" (1 Corinthians 2:9*b,* LB).

Highlights of the pilgrimage include graduating in the class of '40 from the University of Nebraska; Bert S. Gittins national advertising agency, 1940–48; a home-manufacturing corporation, 1948–1957; Kingsberry Homes, 1957–1960; Imperial Homes, 1960–1979; and on call for the Lord 1979–.

The experience of God's helping me come up with answers for fulfilling his call gives great confidence, an affirming conviction for stepping into the unknown future when directed by him.

God Calls All His People

God calls in different ways. It is fascinating to hear people tell of the singular message they received from the Lord, how they received it and where. Some of these divine directions are for the long run; some for an immediate need; and others for the meantime, part of a long-term, unfolding purpose.

Later we will read many, different, fascinating ways in which God reveals a special task for an individual. For an early acquaintance with this variety, let us look quickly at four brief experiences.

My wife, Estelle, mother, homemaker, and my business partner:

> When I was sixteen, a medical missionary from India spoke in our Evangelical Church. As I listened to him, being new in my own Christian experience, I realized I must know more about this man Jesus, who could compel men to give up all to follow him.

I started watching the *Milwaukee Journal* to learn where missionaries were speaking, and if at all possible I would go to hear them and get to know them. It gradually became clear that my call was to the mission field. Unusual opportunities began opening—and to this day keep opening—for me to participate in global missionary work from right here at home.

Belle Blanton, homemaker, Griffin, Georgia:

After committing my life to Jesus, one morning while cleaning our daughter's room, I picked up a Bible lying on the night stand and started reading from First Corinthians, the thirteenth chapter. I could hardly lay it down. This started me on a regular schedule for reading the entire New Testament, then the Old Testament. Every day of reading seemed to be more thrilling than the day before.

Oh, that more people could share my treasure kept going through my mind for weeks. *But how?* I wondered.

In a flash one day, while conducting a women's circle meeting, I saw one way. It was to let church members put Bibles in the pew racks in honor or in memory of dear ones. In about two weeks the project was started. Within a year, 513 Bibles were in the pew racks and paid for, without touching the church budget.

Virginia Law Shell, author:

My call to be chairperson of the Good News General Conference Task Force came through an invitation for me to perform a needed job. This led to prayer, seeking direction from God. On receiving a miraculous confirmation, I undertook the responsibility, with a sense of divine mission, to help change the legislative direction of the world-circling United Methodist Church.

Spencer Bowden, retired technical sergeant, now a mechanic:

My wife, Carol, got me to go to a weekend program in our church, Venture in Discipleship.[1] I was forty-two-years old and living what seemed to be a good and dutiful life, but it was aimless, drifting.

God spoke to me through the words and love of the witnesses that weekend. I responded by accepting Jesus Christ into my life. Then the word came to go out and witness to what Christ had done for me.

Responding, my life suddenly became meaningful and exciting. Next came positions of leadership and responsibility that had never entered my mind.

In different ways, these people tell me that hearing God's call was just the beginning. When they responded, their lives unfolded in unexpected and progressive ways. New directions were received. Life became an ongoing journey with new, ever-expanding vistas that left them in a state of excited anticipation, asking, *What's the next big thing, Lord?* Their answers, and others', unfold in this story, "'You will be told what you must do.'"

Points to Ponder

* Today, as in Bible days, God speaks to his people about serving him in a special way.
* Committing our lives to Jesus Christ is the first step in the anointing of divine direction.
* God calls laypeople, as well as the clergy, to unique areas of service for him.
* Openness and the readiness to respond make his word effective in our lives.
* God's word comes in many ways, often when we least expect it.
* A common pattern is starting with the little call, simply doing a needed job that I can do where I am. "'You have proved trustworthy in a small way; I will now put you in charge of something big'" (Matthew 25:21*b,* NEB).
* Some calls come through a traumatic, supernatural experience. Others through a very reasonable, gradually unfolding process.

CHAPTER 2

God's SOS

Paul lived and worked with them, for they were tentmakers just as he was. (Acts 18:3, LB)

As architect Ed Cheshire drove to work, he reflected again on life's not coming out as expected or the way it could.

In retrospect, he saw himself a seventeen-year-old high school senior at a Baptist church in Moultrie, Georgia, kneeling at the chancel rail. His life and talent were being consecrated to God.

As the people gathered around and prayed, there was a deep feeling that moved within him saying, "Now, once and for all, my life is dedicated to serving Jesus Christ through architecture." It was such a thrilling, memorable experience that even now he could hear the refrain of the hymn they sang.

> I have decided to follow Jesus,
> No turning back, no turning back.[1]

He went to Georgia Tech and majored in architecture, although he just squeezed by. Then came the miraculous acceptance at Harvard, where he got a master's in architecture.

That last year in Harvard was so vivid. He and Judy were married shortly before starting the drive to finish school. They shared God's leading and anointing of Ed's commitment. There was an offer and acceptance waiting for him with the outstanding architectural firm Abreu and Robeson,

Atlanta office. Then came the anticipation of their first child.

Life was unfolding as one would expect, from a dedicated commitment to God.

Climaxing the answer of his boyhood prayers was the firming up of his professional life in Atlanta. And, another dream come true—the chance to locate at St. Simons Island, Georgia. There he discovered the new, Spirit-led Episcopal Church. *How good can life be?* he thought.

Business was growing. Judy was loving and devoted. The children were in good health, growing in charm and graciousness. The church was very spiritual, caring and offering opportunities for service.

But, something was missing. For almost a year, life had been slipping deeper and deeper into a valley, becoming dull and heavy.

That evening he and Judy went out to eat, alone. Judy sensed that he had something on his mind, but she was hardly prepared for Ed's question.

"Judy, what would you say to the idea of my going to seminary and becoming a priest?"

Silence. Finally, "Ed, you know I'm happy if you're happy. If you feel that's a new mountain you must climb, I'm with you. But I don't understand. Holy Nativity has meant so much to us. Everything seems to be going so well."

"Yes, dear, I know. For some reason, a feeling hangs over me that I'm not doing what I could, or should. There's an urge within me to do more for the Lord—to witness more, to be deeper in his service. It weighs on me. Life's luster has paled. I want to get back on top."

"OK, sweetheart. What next?"

"Let's see what the bishop thinks."

Surprise Direction

Father Wright, priest at Holy Nativity, visualizing the consecration of a priest from his parish, enthusiastically set up a meeting with the bishop.

The bishop asked some leading questions. He had obviously prechecked the case. Then he came to the point—brutally, as Ed says.

"Ed, God's greatest need is not for more priests. God's SOS is for committed laypeople, who will witness for him in their everyday life. Remember, God has given you a talent—architecture. You are responsible for using that talent and multiplying it—making it mean more. Your parish, if you wish, can be the people you meet in your business, social, and community life, along with your family."

"By this time," Ed recalls, "I was smarting, squirming in my chair."

The bishop continued, with a new emphasis. "God needs you more as a tentmaker evangelist than as a priest. Priests have barriers in reaching people for Jesus Christ that the laity does not have. People are mostly won to Christ, not from the pulpit, but from someone's caring and sharing—witnessing to God's goodness out of an everyday life.

"Here's my advice to you. You want to do more for Christ? Great. But do it where you are. Go home. Rededicate your life to God. Ask for power to be his witness in your profession, church community, opera, family. You'll discover a joy beyond your fondest dreams."

Ed walked out of the bishop's office stunned but with a new outlook. He shortly experienced rededication and then a determination to carry out the bishop's counsel. There were painful struggles in becoming an authentic, live witness to his contemporaries—that's another story. But, the bishop was right—"Oh, sure, we know him. He's the fellow who's always so happy," replied my St. Simons friends, when I asked if they knew Ed Cheshire.

Save the Church

Today, God's SOS is coming through, being heard. Carl F. H. Henry, lecturer-at-large for World Vision International, says,

> While the National Council of Churches tried to capture lay activity for social change, evangelicals preserved it for evangelistic outreach. Here lay interest has been particularly valuable since clergymen number less than one out of every 200 American Christians, and thus find little opportunity for personal evangelism. Though even the most active programs for lay witness enlist only a minority of evangelical church members, they have brought remarkable evangelistic vitality to local congregations. Many churches consider lay witnessing the next major framework for evangelical advance.[2]

Lay witnesses are credited with reviving the church in the sixties. Ready to give their time and travel expense to spread the good news of Jesus Christ, they went from church to church, participating in the uniquely organized Lay Witness Mission program.[3]

Dr. G. Ross Freeman, executive secretary of the southeastern jurisdiction of The United Methodist Church, gives this graphic report of the spiritual dynamics released through lay witnessing.

> It was out of the troubled sixties that God called into being the Lay Witness movement. Unheralded, a little church in Phenix City, Alabama, tried the idea; then another little church down the road; and another just across the Chattahoochee River. That little drop of a miracle started concentric circles moving across the nation in the pool of disaster and disorganization. The circles got larger and larger and spread from Alabama into Georgia, down into Florida, over into Mississippi, up into Tennessee, and on and on.
>
> Those who were converted became witnesses. Witnesses became coordinators. Thus started a movement of study, retreats, and development that spread through the entire scene. Out of it, God pulled together a mighty army of laypeople who marched across the country at their own expense to see what they could do for the glory of God. . . . I heard Oral Roberts say at Lake Junaluska, North Carolina, "The Lay Witness movement in the sixties saved the church."[4]

Where It's At

The amazing influence of tentmaking witnesses in kingdom building came into sharp focus through the study done by The Institute for American Church Growth. After carefully documenting the data, these almost unbelievable facts emerged: "Over 4,000 people in 35 states and 3 countries were asked why they became part of a local church. 75% to 90% responded that friends/relatives were the 'door of entrance.'"[5]

God's SOS is echoed and reechoed in the familiar story of the well-meaning, six-hundred-member congregation that was shocked at its pastor's reluctant position when it offered to help him. Sympathetic to the incessant demands and long hours under which the preacher operated, the congregation proposed hiring an associate. Good intentions changed to searching self-analysis when he replied, "What I need is, not one associate, but six hundred associates."

Points to Ponder

Committed laypeople

* lead more persons to Jesus Christ—by far—than preachers, evangelists, books, or any other method.
* can renew and rebuild local congregations by sharing and caring with friends and neighbors in a community.
* restore and recharge Christ's church in today's world by witnessing to the glory of God through denominational organizations.
* penetrate all corners of the world by using their talents and occupational and recreational environments to pass on their love of Jesus and faith in God.
* are the group that God needs the most to reach the world today.

CHAPTER 3

NOW

"Come along with me. . . ." And they left their nets at once and went with him. (Matthew 4:19b-20, LB)

"Come . . ." and Matthew jumped up and went along with him. (Matthew 9:9b, LB)

The late Harry Denman became a legend, even as he lived.

Dr. Denman was known and revered by thousands across our land and around the world because of his unusual ability to introduce people to Jesus Christ on a person-to-person basis. Moving through his labyrinth of life—encountering taxi drivers, waitresses, flight attendants, fellow office workers, peers in administration, bishops, janitors—whoever and wherever—he was quick to share Christ. Sensing his love and understanding, people often discovered new life from Denman's on-the-run, person-to-person witness.

Surprisingly, it had not always been this way. In his journal he wrote,

> I was staying in a hotel. The day clerk was very kind to me. The Lord put it on my heart to speak to him about being a Christian. . . . I told the Lord I would do it, but not at that time because there were many people in the lobby.
>
> Two mornings later I came down to the dining room for breakfast. The night clerk was on duty. . . . After breakfast the night clerk was still on duty. I inquired about the day clerk. He said, "We found him dead in his room this morning. He used a gun." I went to my room and begged God for forgiveness. I was trying to

have a revival, and I failed God and this man who had been gracious to me.[1]

Talking about Denman, my friend Jack said as we lunched together, "I would guess that those two would-be disciples mentioned in Luke 9 must have spoken to Denman in a special way."

"Which incidents are those?" I queried.

Jack read from his pocket testament of The Living Bible.

> Another time, when he invited a man to come with him and to be his disciple, the man agreed—but wanted to wait until his father's death.
>
> Jesus replied, "Let those without eternal life concern themselves with things like that. Your duty is to come and preach the coming of the Kingdom of God to all the world."
>
> Another said, "Yes, Lord, I will come, but first let me ask permission of those at home."
>
> But Jesus told him, "Anyone who lets himself be distracted from the work I plan for him is not fit for the Kingdom of God." (verses 59-62)

Commit Immediately

My friend commented, "It seems to me that if there's anything that will insure my effectiveness and being blessed with a life of divine purpose, it is to respond immediately when the word comes to me." His next words seemed to me, at first, reckless, if not irresponsible.

"We may not have the full answer or even the right answer, but the fact that we're willing to commit immediately with what we have and where we are puts us in a position to be directed by God. He'll take us from that point and open up the wonders he has in mind for us." Jack was getting excited.

"Gus," he added, "my new insight is that what happens to me depends on how I respond to God. Look at those contrasting responses to Christ: the conditional acceptance of the two persons in Luke versus the immediate and unconditional acceptance of Peter and Andrew, who left their nets *at once,* of Matthew who *jumped up,* immediately leaving his tax-collecting desk, and of others who responded instantly. Those men offering conditional acceptances lost their big chance, and their names were quickly forgotten. Those who committed when they were called became giants of history, with names living on eternally."

I agreed with Jack as he concluded our discussion, emphasizing, "The key to getting into the mainstream of God's will, as I see it, is to respond now."

As we left our informal luncheon, the picture of a multitalented friend came to mind. He was going through a time of misery. He had been one of the singing stars of our community, but throat trouble had caused him to drop out. Although he was able to continue his professional work, he was lamenting, "I know the Lord has something special in mind for me, but what?"

Some of us, praying for him, were aware of several places where he had been offered opportunities to serve. For one reason or another, he accepted none and continued in his state of bewilderment.

The question came to me: I wonder what would happen if he would take on one of those positions and follow the advice in Ecclesiastes, "Whatever your hand finds to do, do it with your might" (9:10*a*)?

If Jack was right, my friend would probably find purpose in taking on a task the Lord needed to have done and for which he was equipped, even though at first not as self-fulfilling or glamorous as singing.

Then a let-down in my own experience came to mind. My memory brought back the deflation of my pride, an embarrassing memory now. I had been picturing myself as a boy preacher who would sensationally pull in crowds where great numbers of souls would be born again. Instead, the invitation that came to me was to be the secretary of our seventy-six-member country Sunday school. In retrospect, I confess that I took the job because there was nothing better to do at the time. Fortunately, I did not wait for something better later on.

Immersing myself in this assignment and with the understanding support of the Sunday school superintendent, we launched a come-to-Sunday-school campaign. Imagine my encouragement when, after two years, we received the state banner for having the highest percentage of increase in the Evangelical Free Church. It turned out to be a foundation experience, beyond my imagination at that time. It was the first hint that my place in the building of the Kingdom would be in organization and promotion—as a layman.

Wayne Shabaz amplifies the unfolding of his unusual place in kingdom building, resulting from responding to NOW needs.

"Although I had not received a definite call to go into the ministry, the Lord's word was that he would use me as a layman. So, on my first job as a design engineer with Reliance Electric, now part of Exxon, I was open to ways of serving my Master. Of course, there was witnessing in my daily work. Also, the Sunday school in our Assembly of God Church needed a teacher, then a sponsor for the youth. I responded. This led to other things. Participation kept me informed of the needs, challenges, and opportunities of service in our denominational work.

"I heard about our church's receiving letters from Beirut, Lebanon, concerning mission work. In the Christmas season of 1970, a returned missionary showed slides of Lebanon and the ministry. It became very vivid and real in my mind, even intriguing.

"Then, the life-changing call. The words of missionary Bill Ilniski got to me.

"'Hey, Wayne, you're single.' (Either he did not know or had forgotten about my fiancée.) 'You have a profession that would help the economy in Lebanon. Why don't you go, get a job, and then work with me, on the side, in the coffeehouse, ministering to students. Thousands from the Arab world are there. We're at the hub of the Middle East economic, cultural, and social life.'

"Somehow, I knew this was a call from God, and my fiancée, Cindy, agreed. Impulsively, in January '71, without further thought or delay, passage was booked to Lebanon for my bride-to-be and me. Over one hundred résumés, outlining my background, were sent to business firms in Beirut. In April we were married. In June we sailed."

Mysterious Ways

Wayne continues, "Now, we come to a juncture where I learned in my life that 'God moves in a mysterious way / His wonders to perform.'[2]

"As the date of our sailing kept getting closer and closer, I had not received my first offer or even an indication from one firm who might be interested in talking to me. Friends asked, 'Are you going without a job?' We wondered, too. We prayed, waited, listened for an answer. It seemed to be, 'Go. Get a job when you are over there. The Lord will provide.' After all, hadn't God called us? Finally, with nothing in sight, we sailed in faith, believing.

"Then, the test. After six weeks, I had not turned up a single prospect. Money ran shorter by the day. Finally, Cindy and I faced the possibility of returning to the States and of eating our words about the Lord's direction. Surely God would open a door in the final hours before our departure.

"Wrong. We left Beirut with our faith unfulfilled, stress creeping into our lives, wondering where we had misread our call.

"To redeem our time and money, at least in part, we booked our return flight by way of the Far East. At least we could see the sights.

"Our first stop was the capital of Iran, Teheran, a city then thriving and peaceful, long before the bloodshed that would come.

"It was here that miracles started happening. The first day I had five job offers. I ended up joining an American engineering firm. Cindy got a job teaching third grade in a school for American children. Soon we were ministering among fifty young people in a community church, working closely with the pastor, and learning more than we were teaching.

"While headquartered here and traveling in Israel, Russia, and the Far East, the Lord gave me the vision of the vast opportunities for committed Christian laypeople, using their trade or profession, to get into countries closed to evangelistic missionaries. While contributing to the economy and/or society of a particular country, they would witness for Jesus Christ.

"Then God spoke to me about becoming the focal person for recruiting Christians having these particular skills of international demand. From then until now, there have been more experiences of stepping out in faith, unexpected, if not radical, changes in strategies, testings, and miraculous answers.

"By today, the Lord has led me to building an organization capable of consulting and orienting people for cross-cultural operations, serving multinational firms, including some of the largest. We put Christians in countries closed to missionaries. We have offices in Detroit and Houston, with other locations under consideration. As our experience and contacts grow, it's easy to see that the Lord is preparing us for even greater activities ahead.

"God has shown us that, while we accomplish our objectives through a business organization, our primary objective is service for our Lord. With this approach, possibilities continue to explode. Accepting these as God leading and calling us to new ventures, I'm ready to make some more 'impulsive' moves."

I asked, "What if you had not made your first impulsive decision of booking passage, starting your marriage, and taking off without any job—going only on the confident assurance that the Lord wanted you to go?"

"We'd never be where we are. Very likely we would have lost out on our present unique, exciting enterprise. I believe the Lord would have continued to call us and give us another chance. However, if we had not acted when we first heard him beckon, it would have been a big setback—if not a completely different direction. In my opinion," he added, "the key to Christian progress and self-fulfillment is responding to God's needs right away—immediately—when the Lord speaks." That means, NOW.

Points to Ponder

* Often we lose our chance to be blessed and led by not responding at once to God's word to us.
* When we have confirmation, we are to act immediately.
* After we jump up, saying yes to the Lord's call, he then clarifies his direction and unfolds his purpose for us. We don't have all the answers before we start.
* When responding to his call and events don't turn out as expected, we need to go on in faith, believing. This is God's way of leading on to bigger things.
* Joy and purpose for our future grow out of doing what needs to be done where we are with what we have.
* Frustration and disillusionment result from the inaction of holding out for my thing.

CHAPTER 4

Build My Church

And every day the Lord added to their group those who were being saved. (Acts 2:47b, GNB)

"Be sure that you feed and shepherd God's flock—his church, purchased with his blood." (Acts 20:28b, LB)

The meeting was droning along logically, step by step. My eyes were blinking, trying to keep from dozing. The speaker jolted me as his fist came down on the podium and he exclaimed, "It's time for Christians to do something!"

He flashed on the screen a chart, based on a Gallup poll, showing a 17.3 percent decline in regular worship attendance over the past twenty-four years in the U.S. He then added an overlay, based on a FBI report, showing a 105.9 percent increase in the murder rate over the same period. The trend of the crime graph is similar to the reverse of the one on church attendance.

Now, I was awake, furiously making notes. The speaker, Melvin Schell, Jr., president of Church Growth Ministries, Atlanta, Georgia, continued: "The trend of church attendance can be turned around, surprisingly—not by ministers—but by laypeople." He pointed out that ministers usually are a very important part of church growth and that it is recommended the pastor should be involved in teaching and leading the laity to perform the work of the church's ministry.

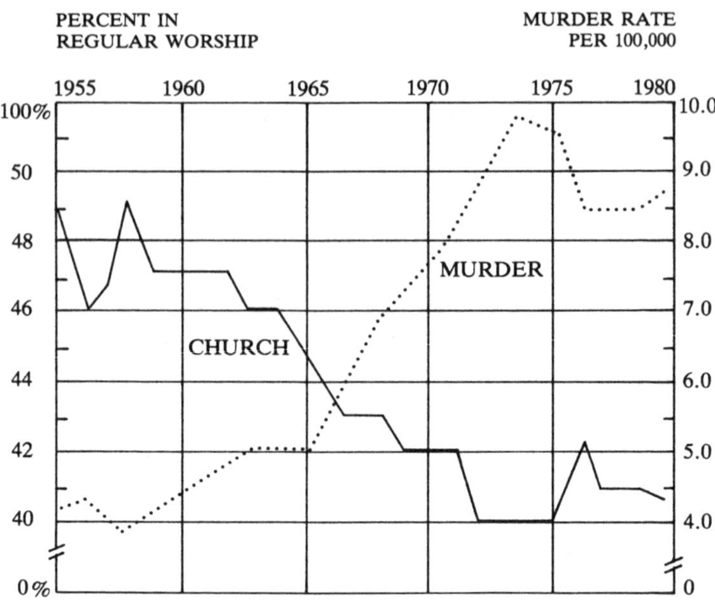

WORSHIP ATTENDANCE, U.S.A.
VS.
HOMICIDE RATE, U.S.A.
1955-1980

SOURCE: GALLUP POLL: 1979-80 RELIGION IN AMERICA;
F.B.I. UNIFORM CRIME REPORT

"But," Schell continued, "invariably, the inside story of a pronounced church growth concerns laypeople committed to sharing the good news of Jesus Christ with people outside the church and then assimilating them into the Christian fellowship.

"This reaching out can come in one of two ways: *(a)* by the laity's taking the initiative or *(b)* by a minister's giving leadership and direction to the efforts of empowered people of the church."

These words set my mind flitting from one corner of the

U.S. to another. In a flash, it was clear that without the men and women in the pew, there might be no church at all—certainly no dramatic story of the Evangelical Free Church of Fullerton, California; the Mequon United Methodist Church, Mequon, Wisconsin; and no behind-the-scene story of our own revived church here in Griffin, Georgia, First United Methodist.

Then came Schell's conclusion, "Almost invariably, where there is measurable growth in a church, from steady to spectacular, there are members sharing the Jesus excitement of their lives as they work on the assembly line, at the bench, behind the desk, on the phone, on the street, in the car pool, throughout the community. They bring in people and build his church."

Laity Essential for Church Growth

"We're going to Fullerton, California," announced my brother, Wesley, telling of the invitation he had received to be the pastor of the church there.

"How large a church is it?" I asked.

"Well, they don't really have a church," Wes explained. "They are renting Sunday rights to a VFW hall. But, there are thirteen tithing Christian families. They have a fellowship going and want to get a church started."

"Where will you live?" Estelle asked.

"They're buying a new parsonage," Wes's wife, Lenore, quickly responded. And, as hoped, the parsonage transaction was closed out, with a $2,000 down payment the day before Wes, Lenore, and their four children arrived.

The first Sunday Wes preached, in March 1956, there were about one hundred present, including children, special guests, and visitors. Twenty-four years later, the congregation had multiplied to six thousand attending two services, with hundreds turned away as Wes preached at the dedication service of the new Fullerton Evangelical Free Church. It contained 100,000 square feet of facilities, including a worship center seating almost twenty-five hundred, an administration/education center, a fellowship center, and a gymnasium.

Let's Pray

Wes acknowledges that, as pastor for thirteen years, he had an important role in the building of this church, but he credits the dramatic growth to the dedication of the laypeople following the timing of the Lord.

A year after Wes arrived, the church faced an expansion crisis. Sunday morning attendance had peaked at about two hundred. The VFW lease was running out and was not renewable.

The planning committee met. A number of options were reviewed, and a dismal conclusion was voiced by one of the men, "We're young and small, and we're planning too big. We better face up to this and admit that our group can't do the job we'd like to do."

For reasonable men, his facts seemed unassailable. The committee was speechless. With no answers, a dead-end silence hung over the group.

Finally one of them spoke up, "I have a family—wife and children. There are other families around here looking to us for a Bible-believing and -teaching fellowship. I believe we've been called to establish a strong testimony. Before we give up on going ahead, let's pray."

After the four men prayed, one of them volunteered, "I can borrow money on my life insurance and maybe on some other things." Another said he would put a second mortgage on his home. Before the meeting was over, the seeming impossible had turned into the likelihood that these four men alone could raise tens of thousands of dollars for starting their own church.

Before they adjourned, plans were made for a potluck supper, where they would share their ideas with the rest of the congregation.

Following this supper, members went out and borrowed on cars, homes, life insurance policies, furniture—anything of collateral value. They sold jewelry, silver, and other items to raise cash. All kinds of sacrifices were made. Thousands of dollars, approaching six figures, were raised among that handful of almost sixty members.

The Fullerton Evangelical Free Church construction program was started. It continued for ten years, expanding from a 3500-square-foot church to one of 15,000 and eventually to the present facility of 100,000 square feet.

Do It Ourselves

John Watson, aircraft engineer, was one of the original praying, planning committee members. Today a successful engineering manager, he says, "We've forgotten how we raised funds for giving us seed money at the bank. Looking back, it really doesn't seem like a sacrifice. What we vividly remember is manually working together to build the church. Everybody worked—men, women, children, and youth. We organized ourselves into teams, with schedules set up according to our occupational hours.

"In the summer, we'd work in the evenings as long as the sun was up. In the winter, we'd turn on the lights. Some teams worked during the day. On Saturdays, we'd work all day, and the place buzzed with activity. Wes and Lenore worked right with us."

John then told how the do-it-ourselves building program continued for about three years. As one phase was finished, it seemed like the steadily expanding congregation would fill it up, and a new phase would have to be started. Finally, the church was able to pay cash for the subcontracting. Then the people teamed up to do other things in the church.

Until Fullerton had a weekly worship attendance of about five hundred, Wes was the only paid staff person. Laypeople volunteered to handle secretarial, janitorial, and visitational duties, church school organization, even associate preaching, and all the other responsibilities of an ongoing and growing church program. Wes's roles were preaching and providing backup for emergencies and leadership for training and organization. He also participated in the building.

"What kind of program did you have to bring in people?" I asked John.

"No formal, organizational program," he replied. "Our activities witnessed so strongly to the community that people would come and see. Our people's enthusiasm in sharing our mission for the Lord made people want to come and be with us. Wherever we worked, we'd tell people about our venture. They came mostly because of our community and person-to-person witness. And we had a follow-up program, coordinated by our pastor and deacons. For interested people, this would lead to membership."

Lay Power

Wes tells me that once people started coming regularly, each new family would be adopted by a church family with similar interests. In this way the newcomers became assimilated into the mainstream of the church. After a time, these newer people also would become shepherds for others, but not until they were accepted into the membership on profession of faith and public witness.

Wes summarizes this lay-inspired program, "It was our aim to keep every member involved in the church's maintenance, programming, and ministry. All members had the privilege of choosing work for which they had a skill, contributing from a few to several hours per week. Ninety-seven percent of our members were involved in the ministry of the church. This generated enthusiasm. At first we did it for survival. Then, we discovered that it was our mission, our opportunity to fulfill his call for our lives. We had a feeling we were using talents that God had given us to do his work. The experience became our joyful witness, even our fulfillment."

Started by Laypeople

Estelle and I can relate to these laypeople building his church. When we moved out to the Mequon, Wisconsin, community, we were driving fourteen miles to First Methodist Church in downtown Milwaukee. Our Congregational neighbors, Homer and Florence Munger, were doing something similar.

"Homer, what would you think of our starting a church here in Mequon?" I questioned.

"A good idea," responded Homer, "but how would we go about it?"

Homer, Florence, Estelle, and I got together. We started praying and exploring possibilities. We talked to neighbors and discovered some other interested people. Then, we wrote a "Macedonian cry" to the Milwaukee District of The Methodist Church. Laypeople from the greater Milwaukee area came and helped us take a community-wide survey.

Then Florence volunteered, "Why don't we start having Sunday school in our home? Each Sunday we'll move the furniture in our living/family room. There we'll assemble. Children and youth classes can meet in our bedrooms. The adults can clean up and whitewash the old summer kitchen for their classroom."

That started it. We organized our group and made plans for getting into operation.

On Saturday, some of us got together to rearrange the Mungers' home. The next day, October 12, 1947, we held our first Sunday school. Thirty-six people made up three classes—one adult, one youth, and one for children.

We started telling others. Slowly, we grew. At the end of our first year, the late Reverend Jim Buxton, then district superintendent of the Milwaukee District of The Methodist Church, offered the part-time services of Alfred Hoad, pastor at neighboring Cedarburg. We were able to commit to a portion of his salary. We had a preacher.

The Mungers' home was now a worship center, in addition

to being a Sunday school. Their sacrifice became the foundation for the building of a new church in Mequon.

In about a year, with partial help from The Methodist Church extension funds, our group had purchased land and contracted for the building of a church. Situated on two acres, it would seat about two hundred and had a basement for the fellowship hall, kitchen, and Sunday school rooms.

Groundbreaking was in October 1948. Our son, Gerrit, then five months old, was the youngest present, and Mrs. William Konig, sixty-eight, as I recall, was the oldest. Our dream became a reality on March 6, 1949, when we held our first service in the church, still under construction.

Then came the big day, September 25, when the late Bishop H. Clifford Northcott came to officially open the new Mequon Community Methodist Church.

The postscript to the Mequon story is that the two acres and the new church soon became too small. Another new church was built at a nearby location. When I visited a few years ago, it had a value of over $800,000 and a membership list of 575. Catherine Collins, one of the original trustees, still living there and currently involved in the church program, says, "As I worked with the small organizing group, walked over two miles, often with our three small children, taught in the Sunday school, and did other things, I had no idea of how the Lord would bless the efforts of that handful of laypeople who responded to God's call to build his church in Mequon."

A New Witness in Griffin

Al Blanton, president of United Cotton Goods Company, with headquarters here in Griffin, Georgia, had his heartwarming experience at our church's Lay Witness Mission, January 1970, when the Lord spoke to him about doing anything Al could to build our local church. From this call, Al went on to become one of the inspired leaders and supporters of the then fourteen-hundred-member body. He taught Sunday school and chaired different committees, finally becoming chairman of the administrative board.

In September 1976, twenty-three men of the church attended a men's weekend retreat, sponsored by our Annual Conference, at Rock Eagle.

"Gus," Al asked, as we were walking to one of the sessions, "what would you think of Belle's and my inviting the men here to come to our home once a week for a simple early morning breakfast? We'd have doughnuts and coffee and a time for sharing and prayer, starting about seven and closing at eight."

"Great," I responded.

Twelve men met that first morning. Seeing all the cars so early, concerned neighbors called the Blantons to see if something was wrong.

The group grew, and nearly everybody offered their home. The first time around, most got calls like the Blantons', "What's wrong?" especially when both a pastor and a doctor were seen at seven in the morning. This early morning group became a community witness. "That's the Methodist prayer group," people explained.

Today this group is two groups, totaling twenty or more members meeting weekly. Prayer, caring, sharing, and the Bible are parts of the experiences. The groups sponsor many key events in the church, such as a Discipleship Celebration weekend,[1] a Walk thru the Bible,[2] and other programs of church-wide and community-wide interest.

At the joint meeting of the two groups, our pastor, Owen Kellum, reported the results of a study being made in Griffin First United Methodist Church, now over eighteen hundred members, "Two-thirds of this group are in top leadership positions in our church. Three-fourths of you are in the top 20 percent of giving. In many ways, you are the foundation of the future of this growing church."

"Al," I asked, "what's your reaction to the result of your original idea of coffee and doughnuts and sharing?"

"Of course, I'm thankful that the Lord spoke to me about

the idea and that Belle was ready to respond with me," Al replied. "As you ask, I'm reminded, we can help build his church right here where we are. Also, the Lord's way of doing things is beyond our imagination. We just have to be ready for and obedient to his call."

Free to Minister

"Fantastic!" "Hard to believe!" "Don't understand it!" "Fastest growing!" and similar expressions kept coming up about Ben Hill United Methodist Church in southwest Atlanta, a transitional community. I pressed Cornelius Henderson, Ben Hill's pastor, for the facts relating to the talk around the North Georgia Conference. "From a membership of four hundred to nearly two thousand in five years," he explained. "Sunday morning service attendance has increased from around one hundred or one hundred fifty to twelve hundred during that same period of time."

My bottom line question, "How do you account for this phenomenon? After all, you have an integrated church; you're in one of the older communities moving from white to black."

"My people are free for ministry. They're excited. They are involved in all kinds of ministry, including, but not limited to, music, prayer, teaching, visiting, administration, men's work, women's work, and I give them their rein. The laity lead others into ministry. I now have a layman who teaches what was 'my' Bible class. Of course, there's much more to be said, such as being an inclusive church, giving a strong proclamation of Jesus Christ, and having a warm spirit, prayer groups, and inspired music. But the real heart of our spiritual growth is our laypeople doing the ministry of the church."

Then he mentioned many names, including Colonel Crawford Russell, Sr., Flo Johnson, Helen Edwards, Reginald Dancil, and Lou Casses.

Crawford Russell, a retired army colonel, uses the experience of twenty-nine years in military organization as a lay leader for Ben Hill. He shares, with the pastor, the leadership role of the rapidly growing Ben Hill church. He estimates that 70–80 percent of the congregation participate in one form of ministry or another.

Lay Evangelism

Mrs. Flo Johnson, a nurse and chairperson of Work Area on Evangelism, explains that her twenty-four members are involved in telephone and personal visitations, bringing people to Christ and to church membership. She gave this insight as to why so many new people come to their church, "Many in our congregation, along with our preacher, are always telling people we meet in everyday life about all that's happening in our spirit-filled church."

She concludes with this telling statement about the influence of the laity in the building of this meteoric church, "We spread the word wherever we are. This brings in twenty-five to thirty new members per month."

Mrs. Helen Edwards, a teacher, and her eighty-five-member group, involved in discipleship development, assume the responsibility for helping new members find their role of ministry in the church.

The mandatory new members' class is under Helen's direction. Laypeople usually teach it, although Brother Cornelius takes his turn. He is always in the class with the new members.

I attended one of their morning worship services the last Sunday in July, normally the dull month of the church year. There were two morning services, fifteen church school classes, including a new members' class, and a special Sunday evening service known as Super Summer Spiritual Revival. When the doors closed that night, about nineteen hundred seats had been occupied, at one time or another, on that Sunday.

To an outside observer, one thing was very evident. During the three assemblies I attended, about fifteen laypeople had a part at the podium in the morning proceedings. They were thoroughly schooled and inspiringly effective. It was a strong emotional experience to see a forty-five-year-old, anointed, deeply spiritual, caring pastor orchestrate the power of committed laypeople for performing the ministry of the church. It is not surprising that Henderson was the recipient of the Harry Denman Evangelism Award.

Points to Ponder

* Committed laypeople are essential to church growth.
* God's great call today is for laity, through whom he can work, to restore his church to power.
* Laypeople are called to take the initiative—not to wait—where spiritual leadership or fellowship is lacking.
* When both pastor and people of the church are deeply dedicated and work together in the building of Christ's kingdom in a community, fantastic things happen.
* Two couples, praying and giving of themselves together, can be the beginning of a rich and and fruitful Christian body.
* Even one person, living in a spirit of prayer, love, and obedience, can change the world for Christ.
* Is the Lord speaking to me about building his church? My answer?

EXPERIENCE II

God Guides

We have just experienced God's SOS. It is for laypeople to serve him through their full-time work and off-time activities. He asks for an immediate response. The urgency is to build "his church, purchased with his blood" (Acts 20:28*b*, LB).

Dr. Lloyd John Ogilvie, distinguished pastor and author, shares this discovery, "The Holy Spirit gives us gifts for each new opportunity and challenge."[1] As we respond to God's call, he gives us daily guidance. He seals our willingness with an affirmation that propels us with direction, courage, and strength, taking us through the unknown and over difficulties. He puts us in the right place at the right time—where life's battles are being fought, with eternity at stake. His substation on earth is our family, in which his power is stored and through which it is released, giving us insights and energy for fulfilling his call.

CHAPTER 5

How Can I Know?

*"Speak; your servant is listening." (1 Samuel 3:10*b, *GNB)*

Andy's question:

"Gus, we need to get together and talk."

"What's the news, Andy?" I queried.

Dr. O. E. Anderson, professor and head of the Department of Agronomy, University of Georgia, Griffin, shared his good news. "I have three opportunities opening up to me, and I'm trying to get direction on which one I should choose. It's not easy. They're all very adequate from the viewpoint of income. There are some differences as to position and responsibility, but all rate well."

He then came to the issue, "My real dilemma is Where can I be of greatest service? Or, put in the language of our sharing group, What is God's will in this choice?"

Charlie's concern:

Charlie Wynn was listening intently, as he leaned against a pew in our church in Griffin, Georgia. Then, he finally unloaded his pent-up concern. "Yes, I know it's an effective ministry and needs to be done. But, I don't have any special feeling about doing it or not doing it. How can I know? As you are aware, my regular pharmacy work leaves only limited time to serve outside my job. For me, it's very important that I have complete confidence—even conviction—that I am using my scarce time in the mainstream of God's will for me."

Virginia's response:

"Who? Me? You have to be kidding. Yes, I will pray about it, but, this time, you must have received the wrong signal from the Lord. However," concluded mother, homemaker, missionary, and author Virginia Law Shell, as she hung up the phone at her home in Potomac, Maryland, "I'll pray."

The common questions among these God-concerned people are, How can I operate with the assurance of fulfilling God's call to me? and How can I know that the call I hear is his will for me?

From the demanding experiences of these friends began a search, in joint discussions and separate inquiries.

How Does God Speak?

The Joy Class, an adult group of about forty members in the First United Methodist Church in Griffin, explored the question How does God speak to us? They came to several conclusions.

1. God speaks to us through the counsel of trusted Christian friends and of our family.

Spontaneous yesses from the class punctuated the sharing of real estate man Tom Barrett, "I got more divine direction for my life from my mother than from any other source."

Someone else commented that personal counsel is extremely important because it is often hard to discern between God's voice and one's own enthusiastic idea. An example was used of a person who thought he had God's word and quickly burned bridges behind him. Two years later he was in bitter despair. He had neglected to consult and to get confirmation, and the result was abject failure.

2. God speaks to us through two-way prayer, in which we raise positive, future-oriented questions, such as *What's your choice, God, for me? How do you want me to use the experience?* Then in quietness, we wait for an answer, which comes, sometimes at that moment, sometimes later.

Lloyd Ogilvie tells that in his experience, "Confident

prayer became 90 percent listening and 10 percent articulating my requests. Thus prayer power becomes an awareness of what the Lord wants us to pray for."[1]

His conclusion grew out of his understanding of the words of the apostle John, "This is the confidence which we have in him, that if we ask anything according to his will he hears us" (1 John 5:14*b*).

3. God speaks as we read and reflect on Scripture and on the experiences of the saints of yesterday and today.

In my case, while weighing the pros and cons of writing this book, a portion of First Chronicles spoke in a special way and successively became to me *(a)* God's encouragement, *(b)* my prayers, and *(c)* God's answer to me: "Jabez called on the God of Israel, saying, 'Oh that thou wouldst bless me and enlarge my border, and that thy hand might be with me, and that thou wouldst keep me from harm so that it might not hurt me!' And God granted what he asked" (4:10).

4. God may speak through dreams and visions.

Ed Robb, the renowned Methodist evangelist, tells of the great author and scholar J. B. Phillips.

> He was going through the night of his soul. The world was looking to the great J. B. Phillips to write another book, and he had nothing to say. He apparently was in deep depression. In this hour of need, C. S. Lewis appeared to him one night. Dr. Lewis had been dead for more than a year. Dr. Phillips had not been thinking of him, and had only met him on one occasion. He gave J. B. Phillips a message and was gone. A few nights later C. S. Lewis appeared again, and gave the identical message and disappeared. Dr. J. B. Phillips arose and wrote one of his greatest books.[2]

One further thought was contributed by Mrs. Allyne Baird, our community's leading Spanish teacher. "We've seen different ways God speaks to us, but we've overlooked the fact that often God speaks to us and we don't hear. Too often, we ignore his words or dismiss the thought and go on our way."

Then, as we were about to leave the class and face the

challenges of the next week, she said something that jolted us to a new sensitivity. "I believe that if we are open to God's speaking, every person here can get a direct message from God—answers or directions or opportunities—through one of the four ways we've discussed. If we just expect and listen, he'll come through."

The Will of God

As Andy Anderson and I reflected on the Joy Class conclusions in order to try to answer his problem of which opportunity to choose, he said, "My problem is multiple voices. Which one is right? Remember, we discovered in our sharing group that the wily, old Devil plants seemingly good ideas to confuse or to create doubt or indecision. I have to sort out the right answer."

We turned to Leslie D. Weatherhead's *The Will of God* and to the chapter "Discerning the Will of God." "I am quite sure that the greatest help available in discerning the will of God is reached when we deepen our friendship with him." Then Dr. Weatherhead set up "signposts" for further direction: *(a)* conscience; *(b)* common sense; *(c)* advice of a trusted friend with Christian insight; *(d)* minds and wisdom of others, with special emphasis on the Bible; *(e)* voice of the church; and *(f)* inner light (God's voice).[3]

Andy's and Charlie Wynn's questions are basically the same, How can I unmistakably know that I'm moving in concert with God's will for me? Weatherhead says,

> To be quite honest he cannot be *certain* until he gets to the end that he won't make a mistake, for he must travel by faith more than by sight. But if he is willing to read the signposts and follow them, he will come out to the place where God wants him to be; and, fortunately, God deals with us where we are.[4]

Open Doors

The telephone call received by Virginia Law Shell was asking her to be the chairperson of the Good News Task

Force for the 1980 General Conference of The United Methodist Church, a political strategy committee.

Virginia has some deep convictions about the doctrinal positions and trends of The United Methodist Church, but church politics—that was something else, a new experience, and at the highest level of lawmaking in the church. But as she promised, she prayed.

"Gus, the Joy Class overlooked one thing," Virginia told me. "I find that often God speaks through opening doors. When doors open, you see or hear of some special task that needs to be done. I've learned, when that happens, to stop, look, and listen, even if I don't understand. My openness to the situation often reveals a particular thing to be done, and it turns out to be my great opportunity to do it.

"Of course," she added, "doors open in different ways, but one of the most common is that of putting a need before us. I like what Rose Grindheim Fisher said in *The Upper Room,* quoting her late husband, 'If no one else is going to do it, if it needs to be done for God, then God is calling you.'[5] Really, it's doing what needs to be done with what you have."

So she prayed about being the Good News Task Force chairperson. Contrary to what she expected, she did not hear a definite yes or no. Instead there were ideas on how she could receive confirmation. Woven into these insights were ways to get the job done. As the Lord spoke to her, she picked up her pen and started making notes. Soon she had five guideposts for direction. They indicated how she could know.

Virginia went back over her notes. Breathtaking. She had to pray once more.

"Lord, it seems impossible. But if I've heard you correctly and you give me positive answers to these directions that you've given me, I'm with you. I'll do it. I'm trusting you. Your will be done."

Fleece Before the Lord

The five directions for checking confirmation of her assuming the responsibility were also five principles upon which Virginia would operate as Task Force chairperson.

1. Her husband, Don, would volunteer to participate in the Task Force leadership.
2. She would work through a committee, and the members would be of her own choosing.
3. The people she selected would unanimously agree to participate.
4. There would be a budget, on which she could start operations.
5. The Lord would show her a way to raise additional funds for ongoing operations.

What happened before she said yes, accepting the assignment?

1. The next morning Don came to breakfast, volunteering his opinion that Virginia should accept the chair and offering to work with her.

2. The Good News group wanted her to work through a committee and was hoping she would elect to choose the members.

3. Every person she contacted enthusiastically agreed to serve.

4. There was a budget sufficient for start-up activities.

5. A plan emerged for raising the money needed to accomplish the objectives of this far-reaching endeavor. In fact, after completing the 1980 task, there was a nest egg for the next General Conference.

Crazy Call?

"Operator, collect and person-to-person to Estelle Gustafson, Fort Payne, Alabama." Standing at the pay phone just off Central Park in New York City, I wondered, *Is this the thing to do?* It did seem right to get the idea to Estelle, as it had just crystallized in my mind. The concept was so far-out for us. Was it irresponsibly wild or for real?

The picture had been developing in my mind for some

time. It started as Paul Schnabel, our financial vice-president, and I worked on the five-year forecast for Kingsberry Homes. We took our work to the president, also chairman of our three-man management committee, of which Paul and I were members.

"Looks good. Let's take it to the board," he said. So, we went to Kingsberry's board. With some slight adjustments, the five-year plan was adopted. Enthusiasm for Kingsberry's future ran high.

At the close of the day-long, tense, and crucial board meeting, I went for a walk, ending up at Central Park. The image came into full color and sharp focus. I couldn't hold it any longer. It had to be shared. Had the time come?

"Estelle, what would you think about organizing and setting up our own home-manufacturing company?"

"Do we have the money?" replied practical Estelle.

"Well, not yet, but I believe we could pull it together if this idea is in the Lord's will for our lives. I'm calling so we can start praying and get either a rejection or encouragement to go ahead." That started our sixty-day prayer vigil.

My call was placed during the latter part of June 1960. The direction we got from our immediate prayer was to take July as a month of continuing prayer. Then we would get either a positive or negative response to the idea.

We discreetly made some basic inquiries. Our banker thought it would be a good idea. He offered to back us with a limited amount of up-front money. A competitive home-manufacturing company proposed that if we would handle sales they would produce homes for us until we could set up our own plant. Cost, price, and margins checked out. Sam Teague, a cherished Christian banking friend, gave us encouragement and advised us on the financial structure for setting up the company. George Bradshaw, a New York financier who had been so helpful to me at a previous company when it needed financing, sounded the only note of caution. "Gus, you're in a good position at Kingsberry. Organizing your own company and heading it up involve taking on a lot of heavy responsibility when you don't have to. Think twice before you do it."

In sum, we felt these were strong confirmations that the call we heard was from the Lord. None of these offers or advice was known before we started our July prayers.

By the end of July, backed by positive responses from the banker, the home manufacturer, and Sam Teague, whose Christian wisdom and understanding we so deeply respected, we had a feeling that the Lord was calling us to this venture in order to better serve him. With the Lord in it, we felt equal to the responsibility about which George had cautioned.

Just to be sure, we took one more month, August, for prayer, listening, and making sure we were hearing right. Our prayer was: "Lord, if we haven't heard you correctly tell us before it is too late. If we have, give us a clear picture of how we will go about this task."

By the end of August, the confirmation was so clear, the call so distinct, I could hardly wait to turn in my resignation and complete the thirty-day notice.

On October 1, 1960, with four children in school (Greg, a senior; Gwen, a sophomore; Gerrit, eighth grade, and Gail, fourth grade, no income, no home designs, no personnel except Estelle and me, no financial backers except the banker offering a limited, short-term loan, Estelle and I signed the legal papers for organizing the company called Imperial Homes.

Foolish? Yes, except—believing the Lord had confirmed his word to us, we stepped out with the confidence that he was leading. Estelle later acknowledged that for a month after the resignation, she had butterflies. As months of organization and preparation dragged on with no income, I, too, had queasy moments. Looking back after seventeen years, when we sold out Imperial Homes, we could see the Lord's hand in every anxious moment—in every day of triumph and in every unexpected turn in the road.

So, how can we know? Dr. Weatherhead succinctly offers

a clear perspective. "Fortunately God can start with us where we are, and he has ways of showing us the path of his will."[6]

Points to Ponder

* God speaks, giving us direction if we listen.
* Satan also speaks to us.
* We must discern between positive and negative communication.
* Reason, God's unique gift to man, along with prayer and Scripture, must be used to evaluate the directions we receive.
* Clear-cut confirmation from God and from trusted Christian friends should be received before committing to a course of action.
* Authentication of our new direction insures us of starting on the right track.
* New directions unfold daily in our walk of faith.

CHAPTER 6

Be Where It's At

*"I am sending them into the world." (John 17:18*b, *LB)*

At 11:13 P.M., the Allied military zone in Okinawa was blacked out. The red-alert siren screeched through the stillness. Suddenly in the pitch darkness, the entire island was astir with activity. Those World War II soldiers in the Pacific were frantically waking their buddies, searching for their clothing and arms, and madly dashing for their foxholes.

PFC Red Bond, Fifth Marine Regiment, First Division Infantry, was sleeping in his jungle suit, under a pup tent near the front lines. Scrambling, he picked up his carbine and ran for his life to a foxhole.

"At the base, I was usually there first. On the front lines, I was nearly always alone," he recalls, thinking of his drive for survival.

I'll Be Your Man

There was a deathly silence in the foxhole. As Red awaited the pending destruction, he crouched low to avoid flying shrapnel. After minutes in the stillness, he heard the dull thud of shells being ejected from the Japanese field artillery and from ours firing back, the noisy engines of planes in dog fights, the cracking ack-ack of antiaircraft guns, and then the shrill whistle of falling bombs, followed by an earth-shaking explosion—and more explosions. The repugnant smoke of the bombs and of the fires reached Red's foxhole.

What will be left of the island? Will the bombs miss my foxhole? thought Red, as he pushed down lower, wishing the hole were deeper. He dared not even glance over the edge to see what was being blown to pieces. Instead, as the seeming eternity of agonizing minutes dragged on, Red found himself praying aloud, "Oh, Lord, if you get me out of this mess and home from this stinking island, I'll be your man. You'll be first in my life. If you'll save me, I'll do whatever you want me to do."

Somehow Red came through that night—and several other nights. And he remembered his vow. In the Tennessee farm country, where he was brought up, a man's word is his bond.

"In those foxholes, I got my priorities straight," says Red and adds, "As my foxhole vow grew on me, I began to wonder, *What does being God's man mean in my life—does it mean preaching?* But something instinctively said that preaching was not for me."

What then? he wondered. Ideas began to emerge.

"The first thing was to live a better life. I had been living pretty rough—cursing, swearing, drinking some, gambling—and tough. For a time, it seemed to be getting me ahead. When I was at home, the telephone company sent me out for days, sometimes for weeks, with a crew of from five to twenty men. At twenty, I was the youngest crew foreman in that part of the country. Now in the military I was living just about the same, maybe even more loosely. Then out of my foxhole experience, I began to think more of my family.

"That really hit me. I knew I had struck it lucky in my marriage. My wife was something special. And my daughter—what a girl. That picture got to me. Thinking in the foxhole, I realized they had been taken for granted. They fit into my life when convenient for me."

Priorities

Red continued, "Over a period of several weeks, that foxhole thinking began to crystallize. It came through to me that, 'to be his man,' I had to get my priorities straight. For the first time in my life, they were clear to me in 1-2-3 order.

1. Do what God wants me to do. Live as he wants me to live. Witness for him.
2. Rear my family. Be supportive. Give them godly training.
3. My job must accommodate my Christian faith and witness.
4. It came to me, as never before, that my spare time is to be used for enriching my life and that of my family—not for self-indulgence.

"Thousands of miles from home, living in daily, deathly danger, my priorities emerged, as neatly arranged as a diagram showing where to plug in the red wire and the black wire."

"So what happened to your life?" I asked.

"That's a long story, Gus." He seemed about to confide, but instead exclaimed, "The Lord gave me what my life craved—action, challenge, even confrontation. You know, I'm an action guy. I like to be in the center of what's happening."

That explanation brought into focus the Red Bond I knew—a nationally known leader in the church; a popular speaker across the country, before many different types of audiences; an influential man in his company and community; father of an outstanding family, whose responses to life obviously carry the marks of Christian.

"Looks simple now," he added, "but it wasn't all that easy. I had some experiences almost as scary as the foxhole, but I knew the winner was on my side."

"What do you mean?" I prodded.

"First," he explained, "I confess that as the bombs let up, the battle died down, and the Japanese surrendered, I didn't do very much to line up my living with the priorities that came to me in the foxhole.

"Looking back, I did one thing that now might seem foolhardy, but it was my first step in adjusting to my new resolutions. I wrote the phone company that if they were planning to send me off for weeks at a time, to give my job to somebody else. I was determined to fulfill my responsibility as a husband and father to my family."

"How about your other priorities?"

"Well, Gus, the war started to wind down. The Okinawa battle was won by June 30, 1945, after eighty-three terrible days of fighting. The first A-bomb was dropped August 6. The Japanese surrendered on August 14. Then, the Marines sent me on a special mission to Peking, which took all winter. I finally got home in the spring of '46. My life hadn't changed much. With the pressure of battle lifted, I lost the sense of foxhole urgency. But those priorities, so etched in my mind, still lay dormant."

"What made them come to life?"

Picking Up the Torch

"My grandfather's funeral—not long after I came home. My grandfather was a clean, godly man, if there ever was one. When I saw the crowds of people, from miles and miles around, coming to pay tribute to the life he had lived, something happened to me.

"After hundreds had come and gone, expressing their appreciation for, and their grief at the loss of, a bright light in their lives, I was one of the last to see his body. Impelled by the impressions of that day, I found myself breathing a prayer.

"'God, with your help, I'll pick up where he left off.'

"My priorities flashed back to mind. That day, I committed to God that with his help I'd follow them.

"After watching the country graveside ceremony and driving away from the peaceful, final resting place, something said to me, 'Red, you're a new man.' And, so it was.

"My life was cleaned up—goals changed, a new life-style, new priorities, new energy, new drive. Everything's been different since. Like Wesley, the father of Methodism, this was my heartwarming experience."

"Do you mean that everything's been going your way?" seemed to be the natural thing to ask.

"No," Red responded. "I can't say that. Although looking back, I'm convinced things have worked out for the best. You see, those priorities the Lord gave me don't always fit in with the world's ideas of doing things."

"For instance?"

"OK. The phone company wanted me to take on a responsibility that meant moving and a lot of travel, breaking down my family life. Turning down that opportunity probably cost me promotions that might well have led to key positions up the corporate ladder.

"Another example. I used to mostly spend my off time in personal enjoyment and socializing. I still do, but in a different way. Now my free time, including many vacations, is used for church work."

Battles—Fun

I began to wonder if that was the way to handle Christian living when he broke in, saying,

"Gus, here's the way it looks to me. Living a Christian life isn't passive. It's active—very active. Part of that is taking a stand for Christ in the world—where you live and perform. You might have to risk your life, vocation—everything—to live by his standards rather than the world's. That sometimes puts me into conflict. When it does, that's probably my strongest witness for him—my finest hour."

Lloyd Ogilvie's words came to mind. "When we are involved in following what he tells us to do, the gift of courage will be there at just the right time. We cannot store up courage; it is given in the raging fury of the battle."[1]

"So that's what happens when my decision-making is guided by those priorities," added Red. "Their nonconformist nature has caused me to lose some vocational promotions and recognitions. But who knows? Maybe the many recognitions and much esteem I have enjoyed as a Christ-committed person far exceed what might have been gained following my ambitions instead of his.

"Those battles are wonderfully rewarding. Life continues to unfold like a beautiful dream. My great discovery is that being in the world for Jesus Christ—where the action is—but not of the world, is the greatest thing that could happen to my existence. I've found it. That's it."

Words from the Lord

At first, however, operating in the world without being of the world was a painful puzzle for me, producing sleepless nights and depressing thoughts of giving up.

A letter to the University of Nebraska from Bert S. Gittins Advertising in Milwaukee, Wisconsin, started the dizziness that left me wobbling in my venture out into the world.

One of the largest agencies in Wisconsin, Gittins handled the Allis-Chalmers farm equipment account, the largest in the state at that time. The agency was looking for a man with an agricultural background, some experience in radio copy writing, and an interest in learning the advertising business for national accounts.

I landed the job and accepted it as a temporary detour from what I thought the Lord had in mind for me—returning to the farm after college and being a farmer. From there, I had planned to go into politics, with an eye on the governor's chair.

But now, this new direction had come. Doors were closed to getting out on a farm. Finishing college, I had no cash to get started. Four younger brothers were on the farm with dad. There was no room for me.

So, was this advertising work a new open door? At first it was hard for me to see. My family could not.

Those words that came to me in the hayrack, crossing the mud puddle in our lane eleven years before, again became my guiding star: "Milton, I want you to serve me in everyday life, where the temptations are the toughest."

"There was no denying," said that inner voice, "this job would be everyday life." And, if the popular book of that day, *The Hucksters,* was a true picture of the advertising world, the temptations would be tough.

The highlights of my agricultural college experience seemed to point toward the Gittins job—the courses in agricultural journalism, in which I excelled; third place in a nationwide contest sponsored by WLW for two agricultural radio scholarships; the strong recommendation for ag radio work from Bill Drip, then NBC director of agricultural radio; the University of Nebraska 1939 essay winner in a contest sponsored by Swift Meat Packing Company; the experience of putting together and giving a weekly farm management radio report on KFAB; a key leader in ag campus student politics; and three times, the top man on the University of Nebraska debate team. These electives and extracurricular activities dovetailed with the communications job. Thinking it would be a step toward getting back to the farm, I took off for a strange, unknown land—the world of agency advertising.

At cocktail parties of sophisticated marketeers and opinionmakers, with a coke in my hand, my ears were especially sensitive to the stories of tricks and manipulations that agency account executives used to win accounts.

"Gotta sell your soul," someone said. "If they want to party, you party. If they want to booze, you booze. If they want slick advertising, that's what you develop. Or if they want to play it straight, then that's your game."

These "insights" challenged me. Gradually, my

confidence grew that I could make my way in the advertising business. But . . .

What about God's way?

What about my life-style?

My mind was haunted with these and related questions, which wouldn't be turned off at night and caused me to toss in restless sleep, meeting the new day with exhaustion.

Every morning seemed to be more confusing than the day before—should I?—could I?—what way should I turn?

The Breakthrough

Searching for an answer, I arranged to have lunch with the late Bert Gittins, the agency owner and my immediate superior. My approach was to ask fringe questions. Should I be joining clubs and entertaining in order to get business? What advice did he have for developing new accounts?

Bert's reply turned out to be my cloud by day and flame by night.

"Gus," he said, "there are two ways to get new accounts. In our business the common one is to entertain big and do a super personal public relations act. The other is to get accounts on the basis of good company relations, merit, and the development of ideas that increase a prospect's or client's business.

"I believe," he added, "that the merit approach is the sound one. Accounts gotten by entertainment are vulnerable and always up for grabs. On the other hand, those based on service and merit are more stable and harder to move."

After this luncheon, words of the late Wm H. Danforth, founder of the Ralston Purina Company, came back to me. At Camp Miniwanca in Shelby, Michigan, he shared with our group of upcoming seniors in college agriculture: "Our most valuable possessions are those which can be shared without lessening; those which, when shared, multiply."[2]

There was the breakthrough. It all cleared up. Gittins plus Danforth gave me this lifeline: While using my talents and abilities in helping businesses grow, my own capabilities will expand. That will secure my future in advertising, not "selling my soul" to get accounts. What a thrilling discovery for a country boy, uneasy about living out a Christian commitment in a strange world.

Merit, service, productivity, company public relations—these became the pillars of my business philosophy. These positive, constructive ideas are consistent with Christian ideals. I could pray and get help—including power—with this approach to competition. How to be in the world but not of it came into clear focus. "They are not part of this world any more than I am. . . . As you sent me into the world, I am sending them into the world" (John 17:16, 18, LB).

This experience left me with visions of my being a winner in "Canaan." Those key words became the platform for my business operations, then as well as later. That kind of business conduct became a witness to the Christian way. Enthusiasm returned. A conviction of being called to be a layman began to grow and strengthen. God was working in my life. The advertising world became exciting and fun.

It Works

About a year after the discovery of how to be in the world but not of the world, I was drafted into military service. Those twelve months had given me time to put this discovery into practice. Did it work?

Coming home from overseas service, forty months later, I received four offers to go back into advertising. In Wisconsin's advertising magazine, Bert Gittins ran a full-page ad, headlined GUS IS BACK!

This exciting endorsement clearly confirmed two fundamental concepts: *(a)* Christian principles work in business and *(b)* a Christian can be in the world but not of it.

What a discovery! Taking hold of these two concepts opened up an exciting career of being a Christian operating in a worldly setting of action, risk, danger, temptation, insecurity, and unfathomable unknowns—but with a divine assurance of being an overcomer.

"'I have told you all this,'" Christ told his disciples, "'so that in me you may find peace. In the world you will have trouble. But courage! The victory is mine; I have conquered the world'" (John 16:33, NEB).

The way the Lord prepared and helped me overcome turns out to be one exciting experience after another—often tense. One of the first surprises comes in the next chapter.

Points to Ponder

* Where's the excitement and meaning of life? It's in the action, the conflicts, the stands we take for what we see as right, the responsibilities we assume to achieve that end—that's where it's at.
* Often we hear God's word for us through the raging battles of life.
* Living in the world is tough and hard, and that's where the Lord wants his people.
* The Lord expects his people to live by different standards from the world's.
* Following Christ's way, we must be prepared to face conflict with worldly ways of life—sometimes, even stand alone.
* Operating on Christian principles, our conflicts become our victories and our witnesses for him.
* The Lord gives us the measure of courage we need to win our battle, big or small.

CHAPTER 7

Family Power

"But all those . . . are like a man who builds a house on a strong foundation laid upon the underlying rock. When the floodwaters rise and break against the house, it stands firm, for it is strongly built." (Luke 6:47-48, LB)

*"A . . . home divided against itself cannot stand." (Matthew 12:25*b, *LB)*

Dr. Sam Vickery tells me: "My medical practice had never been as effective as it has since I made Christ Lord of my life four years ago, as Barbara had done two years before me. Seeing him work in her life, I discovered Jesus Christ. The experience of being Christians together was like coming alive at forty-eight—in both my practice and my personal life."

His wife, Barbara, shares: "Since both of us have become born-again Christians, we find ourselves in the most exciting and meaningful phase of our twenty-six-year marriage. We've been given a purpose for living, such as we never dreamed. Our three children are amazed and supportive, as they see what's happening to us."

These provocative words on life as the Vickerys had discovered it—and for which many of us are searching—made me want to know more.

"What do you mean, Sam? Can you give me a for-instance?"

"Yes, I can," he responded. "It's like this. Before Christ, my life was self-contained, like living in a shell. My attitude was that everything I accomplished was up to me, and to Barbara, insofar as she joined with me. My plans and work were all for me. They were a private affair. Since Christ, it's been the other way—a 180-degree turn."

"Would you mind giving me some specifics?"

"OK, Gus, I'm glad to explain. One of the first changes involved a new feeling of power, of being able to do things I had not done before. It was a good feeling. My enthusiasm for what was happening urged me to share it. I did so on a person-to-person basis. Then Barbara suggested we take a course in lay speaking through our United Methodist Church. Timing being opportune, we took the course. This gave me openings for sharing in churches in our town of Commerce, Georgia, and in surrounding communities. These experiences led me into the Gideons and more public speaking."

Straight in the Eye

"Then a surprising thing happened. As these opportunities for sharing Christ came along, a feeling of confidence in speaking began to flow through me. Almost to my astonishment, I could say what I wanted to say in the manner I wanted to say it. It became easy to look people straight in the eye and tell them, with conviction, what the Lord had done for me.

"This new experience carried over into my work. Increasing numbers of people come to my office for help. Many need spiritual, as well as physical or medical, counsel. For the first time in my practice, I am able to communicate in a one-to-one, direct eye-to-eye manner, regarding the basic issues of life. I can feel the influence of my positive experience flowing into their life. People are responding as never before to my new way of doctoring their ills. It's like having a special power for healing. For me it's a whole new ball game, and it works!"

The Vickery family power grew as they began having daily

Bible reading together. Another new togetherness practice was going to Sunday school and church. Both Sam and Barbara became certified lay speakers, which also added to the common bond.

Barbara mostly uses her training for teaching a Sunday school class. Sam fills pulpits. Whenever possible, the children show up to hear their dad "preach." The family's new ideas about entertainment are rooted in their mutual faith. So what does Barbara mean, talking about family purpose and excitement since she and Sam became born-again Christians? She says, "We've always been a close family and worked and struggled together, but before that morning, four years ago, we did not have Christ in common. Now, as never before, we experience real family closeness and oneness in the spirit, including new power for accomplishment.

"This oneness leads us into ventures such as sharing our faith and experience with others in the community, often through Sam's practice; guiding his patients toward new hope and life; speaking and teaching in our church and neighboring churches; together going to different places on Lay Witness teams sharing Christ; seeing men, women, youth, and children become committed and renewed spiritually; meeting stimulating people; going out as short-term medical missionaries to poverty-stricken sections of Jamaica; and, best of all, having our children affirm and encourage us.

"Yes, since we put it all together with Christ, we've had more fun, adventure, and fulfillment than ever before. It does things for a family."

The Whole Family

Hearing Sam and Barbara tell how Christian togetherness had empowered their call, another couple came to mind. They have been in the national spotlight of evangelism for some time. Knowing they have to make a day-to-day living in real estate sales, I was puzzled as to how they could do it.

Real estate broker "Daddy" Doug Strickland says, "Without my family with me all the way, I would not be able to fulfill my unusual, across-the-country, and into-the-world ministry; nor would I be able to successfully handle my real estate business here in Haddonfield, New Jersey."

June, who is a real estate broker, secretary, wife, and mother, responds, "With our whole family called by God, he has led us and given us togetherness and adventures such as—it seems to me—few families have been privileged to experience. And, this wasn't done by going on exotic vacations or hideaway family weekends. It was done by being open and responsive to God's opportunities for our lives."

"How did it start?" I wondered.

"By being the chairman of a Lay Witness Mission," said Doug, "while we were living in Kentucky."

During the busy weekend of the mission, as Doug heard men and women share their enthusiasm for God and Jesus Christ, the idea gradually grew in his mind that Christ had to be supreme in his life. Then it got next to him. Sunday morning when the altar call was given, he responded, ready to give Christ first place, whatever that meant.

As Doug responded, June, too, was with him. Having been occupied with the many demands and activities of the weekend, they had not discussed their deep, personal reaction to what was happening. But it surprised both of them that they were ready to make the ultimate commitment of their life.

With Doug and June at the altar that morning were their children—Jan, sixteen, and Alan, thirteen. It was the beginning of the Strickland ministry. The whole family had been called. What came out of that call is a story of great human accomplishment. Doug says that only by divine power does it come true.

The start was simple enough. All four began going on Lay

Witness Mission weekends. Then Doug started coordinating missions. The family went wherever they were invited, usually within a two-hundred-mile radius, sharing the joyful news of the lordship of Jesus Christ in their lives.

Next, Doug was asked to be the regional director of Lay Witness Missions for the six states of Ohio, Illinois, West Virginia, Indiana, Kentucky, and Michigan. That meant, not only going on missions, but recruiting, training, and assigning coordinators for the whole area. The venture quickly expanded to the extent that Doug and June set up missions in 750 churches in 1973. Doug did the up-front work, June the secretarial work. She comments, "Our home became Grand Central Station, with preachers from all over the area calling and with coordinators, missioners, and Lay Witness officials from far and wide calling and stopping by to see us and stay with us unexpectedly, at most any hour of the day.

"In the middle of all this, we were blessed with our third child, Holly. She went with us on missions while I was pregnant and when she was a baby. The Sunday after she was born, there were several churches over the country that mentioned her in their bulletin and had a rose on the altar for her. And, she grew up in missions."

The upshot of these more than fifteen years in Lay Witness Mission work is that thousands have given or recommitted their lives to Jesus Christ. The ministry of the Stricklands by now has been felt in forty-six of our states, as well as in South Africa, England, Ireland, and Switzerland. Moving to New Jersey from Kentucky extended the core of their ministry from the north central and southern areas of the U.S. to the east coast. Over two hundred missions have been coordinated personally by Doug and June. Their training and recruiting hundreds of people attest to their devotion. They have initiated Lay Witness Missions in prisons, developed organizational guidelines, helped shape policies, and had a large part in church renewal.

How were they able to accomplish all this? Virtually at

their own expense. In the heat of scheduling the 750 missions, June was a real estate broker, mother, homemaker, and Lay Witness Mission secretary. Doug was building homes, being a broker-partner, building up a three-office real estate firm with thirty sales people, and teaching real estate courses.

"We don't even try to explain it," says Doug. "We believe that God leads us in our business and in our mission work. Sometimes anxiety creeps in as to how expenses versus income are going to work out or time is going to stretch. When that happens, we pray—often on the run. Then we relax, and somehow it works out. Actually, we're relaxed people. Even better, we're blessed people. Our family is close, and we have a great rapport.

"I'm usually one of the top producers in our organization of about three hundred sales people. It's strange, but it seems that when we return to work on Mondays someone is ready, if not waiting, to buy a home. Our associates, neighbors, and local church people are very understanding of our situation and are helpful and supportive, for which we are humbly grateful."

Then Doug made his declaration of dependence. "Without my family—children who not only understand but participate and encourage, and a wife who is as much a part of the work as I—we'd still be drifting and groping. My family makes it possible to fulfill my ministry. Yes, more than that, they make it possible to fulfill our ministry."

Turning to June, I wondered about her response—she being a caretaker of the family, so often on the receiving end of abrupt changes, unexpected guests, and time squeezes, managing the household budget, and filling in as secretary of the company and of missions coordinating.

Her evaluation: "I stand in awe of the opportunities God gives us and helps us accomplish. I'm thankful for the abundance he provides, making it possible for us to do these things. I'm amazed at how he equips us for meeting the challenges. Many times, it seems impossible. My encouragement often comes from a reminder given me by a dear friend, early in our experience, saying that God is more concerned about our availability than our capability. So we live open lives, flexible and ready for any new thing God has for us. Awesome? Yes. Rewarding? Beyond imagination."

My own reaction is like Doug's as I look at the impact of family faith on the fulfillment of God's purpose in our lives. Without my family—particularly Estelle—my calling probably would not have gotten beyond the hearing stage. Certainly, these lines would not be written, and Estelle would not be typing them. Even while I struggled to adjust to the advertising world, Estelle was giving me encouragement.

As we courted, bicycling along the shore of Lake Michigan and enjoying activities in many beautiful places in the Milwaukee area, she would listen to my dreams. She had a way of making them bigger and more real. It still amazes me that as time went on, she was willing to take on my dreams and to make them hers. That took someone special. At the same time, her dreams became mine. She became a part of my spiritual life and expanded its dimensions. Our lives were being deeply anchored for the risks ahead. These came sooner than expected.

On August 1, 1942, the day of our marriage, I received, from Uncle Sam, a letter summoning me to military service. Thirty days later, shipping orders from the draft board sent me to the Great Lakes Naval Station for induction.

For twenty-one months there was a series of Air Force school and service assignments stateside. After each assignment was made, Estelle would come and find work and a place where we could live together.

Then in late April 1944, I sailed for the South Pacific. On May 9, while I was on the high seas, one day out of Sydney, Australia, our first son, Greg, was born in Nebraska. Five battle stars and nineteen months later, Estelle left me alone with Greg for the first time, in a hotel room in Hastings,

Nebraska, for a couple of hours. It was as frightening as some of the foxhole experiences.

The war years strengthened our faith and marriage. While in this country, we always found a local church where we became temporary members. We participated as though we were permanent. These churches welcomed, loved us, and opened their heart. It was an uplifting, stabilizing experience to learn that with God's people you're never a stranger. As time went on, we found this true around the world, regardless of race or economic status.

Long-Distance Devotions

While trooping the country, we had time to read and share daily devotions. This was the beginning of a practice that steadied and strengthened us as a family over the years ahead. Even when we were about ten thousand miles apart for those nineteen months I was overseas, we had our daily *Upper Room* devotions. I would often have mine at the same time I knew Estelle was having hers, adjusting for the time difference and depending on my duty situation. In our daily letters, we shared thoughts that came to us out of the daily devotional discipline.

When the war ended, we entered the readjustment period with a stronger faith and marriage than ever before. We were spiritually and maritally equipped for many opportunities, hazards, and unexpected turns that awaited us in the fulfilling of God's call for our lives.

Going through the war years, we were not fully aware of how the Lord was leading. Today, it is obvious. He was using circumstances for molding and bringing us together as a family unit.

Like the Vickerys and the Stricklands, although in a different way, we found our family had to be as one before my calling became really effective. And there was something different—stronger, more exciting—we, not just Gus, were to fulfill his calling.

It has been thrilling to uncover this great truth: In God's beautiful design for the most effective living, the family is first. This adds an exciting dimension for accomplishment—family power.

Keenly aware of our many failures, we are filled with gratitude and surprise to see how Christ, the ideal and hope of our marriage, uses us in ways beyond our imagination. There are heartaches, defeats, and setbacks. But, with him, we have learned that frustrations are elements in making us winners. And life is much better when our family works, plays, and prays together. Finally, we discover, as we move to our next experience, that we are ready, with God's help, to tackle the impossible.

"What is impossible for man is possible for God" (Luke 18:27*b*, GNB).

Points to Ponder

* A personal commitment to Jesus Christ by both spouses generates supernatural family power.
* One's ability to fulfill a call is greatly enhanced when backed by a Christian marriage and family.
* The common bond of Christ between husband and wife makes daily living more joyful and effective.
* Christian family disciplines strengthen marital and family relationships.
* The high-level motivation of the Christ-centered family is rooted in the unique values and priorities of faithful Christians.

EXPERIENCE III

God Empowers

We discover that as we answer God's call our power grows. Our first encounter is one of urgency—SOS and NOW.

As we respond, he equips and guides—puts us on track for great accomplishment of his objectives for our lives.

Like the butterfly that breaks out of its cocoon, we are empowered to break out and move away from things that would hold us back. Divine resources continually unfold to meet the demands of our upward-moving growth levels. This fountain of power and wisdom gives us energy and direction for meeting every challenge on our road to fulfillment.

CHAPTER 8

"Enlarge My Border"

Jabez called on the God of Israel, saying, "Oh that thou wouldst bless me and enlarge my border, and that thy hand might be with me, and that thou wouldst keep me from harm so that it might not hurt me!" And God granted what he asked. (1 Chronicles 4:10)

As a fourteen-year-old boy, David W. Brooks chose to work in the cotton fields of his father's farms, rather than in his father's store. He preferred the company of the simple sharecroppers to that of the pool-hall crowd. Walking behind a mule and plow or chopping weeds stimulated his thinking. His mind searched for answers to the poverty of those farmer friends of his, as well as to the future of Georgia farming.

At sixteen he enrolled in the University of Georgia. There was no question, no doubt, that agriculture was to be his field of study. That was his call.

Answers and Direction

Through his studies at the university, he began to find answers to many of the questions that had troubled him back in the fields or by the stream. His discoveries were so exciting he hardly took time to eat and sleep. He immersed himself in agricultural science and economics.

His diligence earned him a bachelor's in agricultural science at nineteen, within three years after his enrollment.

With the degree came a position in the Agronomy Division of the University of Georgia. The youngest professor on the staff, he also studied for his master's degree, which he received at twenty.

The more he taught, the more he was convinced that he had an answer to the farmers' dilemma. The key to changing the future of agriculture was through the upcoming county agents he was teaching. He poured out information for them to take to the counties where they would be stationed. In this way the economics of farming would be changed.

Professor Brooks' prescription: good, appropriate fertilizers, improved seeds and insecticides, and financing to make them possible.

The response to his fervent, inspired teaching was enthusiastic. He watched for field results. There were signs, but they were so slow. He was looking for quicker results. Finally, a definite plan took form—Get out and do it instead of telling others how. He had a choice of going in either of two directions.

Word got around about that professor at the university and his ideas for turning Georgia agriculture from poverty to prosperity. Some financiers offered to back him in a business that would help accomplish his objectives. This would undoubtedly have meant a fortune for David Brooks. But this temptation only fired the idealism of this young crusader. As he grappled with this lucrative offer, it became clear that he was more interested in solving the plight of the farmers than in making himself rich.

Five progressive, but poor, farmers also recognized the possibilities of Professor Brooks' agricultural economic ideas. They asked him to organize and manage a farmers' co-op for them. They offered him a $5,000-a-year salary. He said it was too much and recommended only $2,400 in order to ensure the success of the embryonic Cotton Producers Association, later to become famous as CPA, and eventually as Gold Kist.

So at twenty-three, against the advice of his father, David, known as D.W. now, walked into the university president's office to resign from his professorate. His father's reaction was mild compared with the president's. After failing to win him back by reaffirming the excellence of his work and his bright future in the university system, the president became flustered, then angered. The brashness of this fair-haired upstart appeared irresponsible, ungrateful, and unreasonable. With his blood pressure rising and his face becoming redder by the minute, even hammering his fist on the desk, he lectured D.W. about his ingratitude, lack of vision, and starting a venture doomed to be self-destructive.

D.W.'s response was that there were already thousands of farmers failing, so one more would not make much difference. In his own mind, he was confident.

Catching the Vision

Little did D.W. realize that the risk he was taking would lead to his becoming one of the twentieth century's most respected fighters of hunger and poverty. Seven U.S. presidents, Truman through Carter, sought his advice on food production and distribution. India's food famine of the '50s and '60s was turned into a surplus under his direction, along with the help of nine other co-op leaders from America. Even the Russian and Chinese ministers of agriculture have requested his advice. Distribution of U.S. farm products has been set up by his visiting and opening marketing doors in a hundred foreign countries. All the time Georgia's, then southeastern, farm production, was increasing two-, three-, four-, fivefold, and more. Georgia's farmers' cash income went from $72 per year in the early 1900s to an average of $52,000 for '78–'79.

To get Cotton Producers started, D.W. barnstormed Georgia. Usually the county agents would bring together an audience. He got the farmers' attention by hitting them hard. His opening remarks usually started: "You deserve what you have—no shoes, one patched pair of overalls, one ragged shirt, no food stored in your pantry. You aren't producing, and you aren't doing anything about it. You could if you wanted to. But your wives and children can't, and they don't deserve the kind of life you're providing."

Some misunderstanding farmers labeled D.W. mean. Others asked, "What can we do?" He then held out the program of cooperative production, the purchasing of high-quality fertilizer, seeds, and insecticides, and proper application, along with cooperative marketing.

For a called meeting of all members of the Cotton Producers Association, after getting the new operation underway, 8,000 showed up at the headquarters in Carrollton, Georgia. The plans for an indoor meeting had to be changed to outdoors. No facility was big enough to handle the crowd. Along with "cracker" baseball, the first CPA meeting was one of the big events in Georgia in 1934. Farmers began to have hope.

Following the Carrollton meeting, life began to explode for D.W. His character attracted opportunities wherever he went. It was a most unusual one, being ingrained with the example of a compassionate mother, the imperative of a Christian conscience, the methodology of a scientist, the probing analysis of a financier, the persuasive enthusiasm of a star salesman, and the energy of a dynamo.

Stories are told of his catching a plane at 4:30 A.M. in some remote part of the U.S., arriving in Washington for an 8:30 meeting, and flying back to where he started for a late-afternoon or night meeting. While traveling, he would recruit people to join his crusade. And so the stories go.

Seeing the Results

First in Georgia and then across the Southeast, the landscape became marked with Farmers Exchanges, grain-buying and -processing facilities, fertilizer plants, feed-manufacturing plants, broiler and egg production facilities, poultry processing plants, hatcheries, peanut warehouses, and other agricultural product centers. Finally, offices and plants were set up around the world.

Today, Gold Kist is the second largest industry in Georgia, next to Coca Cola; ranks as number 193 on *Fortune*'s list of the 500 biggest industrial corporations; and is the 48th largest exporter in the U.S. Sales have grown from approximately $100,000 in the first year of operation to nearly $2 billion today.

Mr. Brooks' Christian dedication and his faithfulness to The United Methodist Church elevated him to top positions of church responsibility. Bishops would often call on him for personal advice and direction. Methodist-related Emory University awarded him an honorary doctor's degree. Many people know him as Mr. Methodist. He became vice-chairman of the Board of Global Missions. While he was opening up marketing outlets around the world during the day, his wife, Ruth, would work with missions in that particular country. At night, Ruth and D.W. together would hold meetings with the missionaries. Thus, they knew, and were in touch with, Methodist missionaries around the world.

As the worldwide enterprises of CPA became highly profitable for its members, increasing pressures were put on D.W. to turn his money-making ability to personal gain. One group went so far as to charge him with having a moral responsibility to use his business acumen in building up a big estate for his wife and children.

D.W. replied, "I have to determine my own moral rights. If you would give me a million dollars a year now, I wouldn't take it. This is what I want to do. Gold Kist helps lots of people who, I think, need financial help. Most of them were at the bottom of the economic ladder. Now they're on the road up. And Gold Kist will be here long after I'm gone. I have all the money I need, maybe more."

The late United Methodist bishop, Arthur J. Moore, D.W.'s bishop for twenty years and pastor for a time, knew well the philosophy and faith that motivates this man of international accomplishments. Bishop Moore, also a world-famous personality, said of Mr. Brooks, "I have known of no man who exhibited in his daily living a finer type of consecration of character and unselfishness than I have seen in this man. . . . Everything in the church and in the state has been made finer and better and more useful because of the consecrated leadership of this noble layman."[1]

Recently while driving over an improved country road, successor to the wagon rail of the boyhood days of eighty-year-old D.W., a modern four-wheel-drive pick-up truck passed him. He noticed the bumper sticker—I'm Proud to Be a Farmer.

It prompted memories of the lonely day he walked out of the University of Georgia president's office, a predicted failure. He breathed a prayer, thanking God for giving him vision, the courage to do, and the courage to intervene when bad mistakes were in the making. He was grateful for the privilege of giving farmers hope and a sense of pride, of making fields produce abundantly, of filling pantries with food, and of putting shoes on the feet of the people in Carrollton and around the world.

Recognizing Talents

Another hunger fighter, reaching around the world, is John Bass, a Presbyterian from Oconee, Illinois, now headquartered in Colorado Springs, Colorado. He fights a different kind of hunger—spiritual hunger. Like D.W., he does it as a layman through the private enterprise system.

"If I had listened to my preacher friend," says John, "I would have missed the thrilling experience of God expanding my lay ministry from Decatur, Illinois, to world dimensions. Although what he did was done in a spirit of love, he came close to disrupting my calling. His pressure on me to become a preacher and leader in the Baptist denomination almost caused me not to recognize that my talents were in the business field and not in the pulpit."

These arresting words came from a man whose gift is

administration—acknowledged by Scripture (1 Corinthians 12:28)—and is being used today by more than thirty-eight hundred Christian bookstores in the U.S., Canada, and other places in the world. More stores are steadily being added.

"John," I asked, "was there a specific moment in your life when you heard God say that you were to be an administrator for him?"

"Not exactly. It was an unfolding process, but one day I saw with conviction that God had given me a special talent to be used in a special way for him."

Forgiving

John's story of being led to Christian commitment covers a period of about five years, starting on the U.S.S. *Mt. Olympus,* flagship of the Third Amphibious Fleet Command, during World War II. He served as chief personnel yeoman on Admiral Richard E. Byrd's staff.

Anchored off the Philippines, shortly after General MacArthur's return, he witnessed the release of inmates from the infamous Japanese prison camp Santo Tomas.

Seeing the inhuman conditions and atrocities under which the prisoners had lived, he was inflamed and indignant—starvation diet, cruel treatment, filth, indignities, and torture. He recoiled in disbelief and revulsion as he watched the walking skeletons, stumbling and dragging themselves through the opened prison gates. His teen-age mind was filled with hate for the Japanese. He saw them as enemies of human decency and rights.

This hate lingered on after the war, while he studied and even as he moved into the opportunities of his challenging career. The picture of suffering, degradation, and debilitation would not be blotted out of his mind. He detested the Japanese.

Then one day he saw a newspaper notice that missionaries, survivors of Santo Tomas, were going to speak in Decatur.

Curious as to what they would have to say, he and his young bride went.

What they heard was hard to believe. The missionary team spoke about their love for the Japanese and about their desire to go to Japan with the good news of Jesus Christ.

This contradiction to the hate in John's mind was disturbing. He left the lecture with a feeling of uneasiness, even bewilderment. The example of the love of these missionaries, motivated by Jesus Christ, began to dislodge his deep-rooted hate. Finally it happened—John was able to pray, "Lord, forgive me. Clean out my hate. Forgive my sin. Replace it with love for all people—even the Japanese—as I saw it in those missionaries. Would you, Jesus, come in and be the center of my being?"

Using Talents

He surrendered to Christ. New purpose and meaning replaced his hate feelings. He began to evaluate life in terms of Jesus Christ.

Reevaluating his journey of twenty-three years, he felt reasonably sure of one thing: Personnel was his line. His direction was related to his experience working on Admiral Byrd's staff with personnel selection and assignment. He had loved it.

Upon returning to civilian life after thirty-three months of service, he headed for James Milliken University at Decatur, Illinois. There he studied more about personnel management and business administration.

Recognizing John's intense interest in these fields, Wagner Malleable, located in Decatur, recruited him. Even before he completed his degree, he was Wagner's personnel director.

Two experiences here changed the course of John's career. Wagner is a well-managed and competitive company in the steel business. In this setting John developed a keen business sense. Working hand-in-glove with the company president's closest advisors, his young, searching mind absorbed principles of successful business management, hard to get except in such circumstances. Wagner gave him a loose reign for moving ahead, including public relations assignments at sales meetings, cocktail parties, and other goodwill-building events. The cocktail parties left him uncomfortable. But with expanding responsibilities, including a new title of industrial relations director, he felt he was finding a niche for himself in the business world and had a growing understanding of what it was all about.

During this time, a Baptist minister had a great influence in John's life. The minister stressed the satisfaction and joy of using a person's talents in God's service. It gave this young businessman an urge to do so. The minister also pushed him to enter the pastoral ministry.

"However," John says, "something held me back. But the minister's challenge kept returning to my mind for some time."

God Calling

At this point John attended a Christian Businessmen's luncheon in Decatur, where an administrator of the R. G. LeTourneau earth-moving equipment company declared, "Christian organizations are bankrupt of management leadership."

Then he explained that ministers, not trained in business management principles, are called on to manage Christian enterprises. He challenged business people to fill the gap.

"That was the answer to my dilemma of the urge to serve but no deep conviction about being a pastor," explains John. "However, there seemed to be no opening for me in the business management of some Christian organization. At the same time, it was easy to see God's moving in my life. He was blessing my work with people. He quickly brought me the opportunity for putting my training into practice. Then he showed me the possibility for a sacred kind of secular service, right in line with my talents." Then, the exciting opening. "It always comes when God gives you a vision," John maintains.

A local Decatur minister learned that Tennessee Temple Schools, a new, conservative Christian College at Chattanooga, Tennessee, needed a personnel manager. Aware of John's enthusiasm for Christian service, the minister suggested a contact. John got the job, and, with it, an opportunity to complete his degree and to teach two courses.

While John was teaching, two Moody graduates in his class took special note of this young professor and his way with people. They secretly arranged for an interview with the Moody Foundation, the business entity of the famous Moody Bible Institute. John agreed to the interview. Moody added him to the staff.

At first, John's personnel and business administration talents found expression as the nonacademic personnel manager of the Moody Foundation. Later, the academic enterprises were added to his responsibilities. Next, being budget director of the entire Moody complex was added to his office of personnel management. He could see the fulfillment of his Decatur luncheon table call—Christian organizations need Christ-committed professional business management.

Many would say he was sitting on top of one of the largest, most far-reaching Christian organizations in the world. "But seemingly," said John, "the Lord had different ideas—as long as I had an open mind and was willing to respond to the Lord's leading." Hidden in the future were vast horizons.

John's management-training program at Moody became widely known. The Christian Booksellers Association (CBA) requested Moody to permit John to come on a temporary basis and set up a management program. Moody approved, and during a two-month period in 1961, John developed a management-training program for CBA.

In 1965 CBA approached John about becoming their executive vice-president. For four years he had been keeping an eye on CBA. Compared with his responsibilities at Moody, it was very small. At Moody there were 585 full-time employees and 350 part-time, plus a budget of millions. At CBA he would have a staff of one full-time secretary, one bookkeeper, and himself.

"How could you even be challenged?" I asked.

"At first, it was hard to see, realizing the miraculous way the Lord had led me to Moody's and the tremendous opportunities for Christian service with them," explained John. "But, again, the Lord, in his own way, led and prepared me.

"After I set up the management-training program, Moody allowed me to help CBA from time to time, with other problems, including the leadership of management seminars. The potential of their business began to be apparent.

"In the course of this experience God gave me two specific insights about the store owners: *(a)* their deep spiritual dedication to spreading the gospel through Christian books, often risking their savings or selling or mortgaging their home; and *(b)* their need for good, professional management to enlarge their ministry.

"Another insight probably should be mentioned. It seemed that God had particularly equipped me for furnishing CBA with the pattern for the kind of management skills they needed. I knew both small and big business, the book business, publishers, and book-marketing. As he did in other things, it seemed as though when I prayed to do the right thing, the Lord led me to the door and said go in."

Expanding Borders

The validity of that experience sixteen years ago is now history. Compared with 1965, the average annual-dollar-volume of sales per store has increased from approximately $38,000 to a present $145,000, with some having as much as $500,000 to $1,500,000 in one location. The pattern of stores coming into the association is that, after joining, their annual sales steadily increase. The annual increase often runs from 5 to 6 percent more than that of the big chain stores. Bass feels this is due to the motivation of the private entrepeneur. Also, many association members credit association management services with success know-how.

The association has an annual national convention. Current attendance is up to eighty-five hundred, with a thousand display booths covering five acres.

The number of member stores has grown from roughly seven hundred in 1965 to thirty-eight hundred in the U.S., Canada, and now overseas, including Australia, New Zealand, Singapore, South Africa, East Africa, and Zambia, adding up to more than a 500 percent increase in the past sixteen years. The numbers increase annually.

"Equally important," says John, "is the updated community image of the Christian bookstore. So often in the past, the store was on the owner's porch or in the basement of a church or in a back alley. Today 91 percent of the stores are on the main street, or in a modern shopping center.

"We believe," he adds, "if it is the Lord's work, it should be done right."

"It must be pretty clear today why the Lord led you to move from a setting of hundreds of people and a budget of millions to a staff of three and a budget of a few thousand," I suggested.

"Yes," responded Bass, "but I discovered that God was moving me into the large family of totally committed, surrendered Christians, willing to risk all for Jesus Christ. What this means to me is that I'm not just an executive with a staff of twenty-nine. Instead, I, my staff, and the owners and managers of over thirty-eight hundred Christian bookstores, scattered around the world, are one in spirit, with one objective: to answer God's call for the professional, skilled management of a Christian mission that extends his word into the lives of both non-Christians and nonreading Christians. They're hungry for the real thing. We're out to replace meaningless or worthless reading with Christian reading that is life-giving and life-renewing. As we continue to follow God's leading, there's no end to the enlargement of our borders."

Points to Ponder

* Important parts of our call are to expand our capabilities and to assume greater responsibilities.
* If we are willing to be used by God, he takes the talents we have and enjoy and uses them to his glory and our fulfillment.
* Divine enhancement of our call comes by putting ourselves in the Lord's will, doing the work he wants us to do, and then praying for guidance and blessing.
* Once God shows us his purpose for our lives, it becomes our responsibility to *(a)* fill every hour with productive, constructive, life-building effort, and *(b)* train, employ, and exercise our God-given talents to the limit.
* The Lord requires risk-taking on our part to work with him for accomplishing his purpose in our lives.

CHAPTER 9

24 Hours—7 Days—52 Weeks

*"Go home to your friends . . . and tell them what wonderful things God has done for you." (Mark 5:19*b*, LB)*

"I nearly fainted walking back to my seat, realizing what I had just done," says John Woodall, president and treasurer of Woodland Furniture Manufacturing Company.

For fifty years John's attitude toward religion had been to play it safe. Growing up in rural Woodland, Georgia, population 750, he believed the hellfire preaching of his early days. He wasn't going to get caught. His strategy was to live a good life and to do good work, particularly in the church.

So, as John says, "During my first fifty years in the Methodist Church, I was trying to earn my salvation. Then in March 1974, some peanut farmers from Donalsonville, Georgia, held a Lay Witness weekend in our church. During that time, it became clear to me that salvation is a gift of Jesus Christ, not something you earn by good works. That really upset me. My fifty-year strategy went down the drain.

"I also realized that the gift was given to those who put Christ first in their lives.

"By Sunday morning, after sharing with those people from south Georgia since Friday night, my spiritual views were reversed. Then, too, the love and joy in the lives of those missioners really touched me. They had something. It looked like the real thing.

"Sunday morning when the mission coordinator called for

those who wanted to make comments or commitments, something in me said, *John, go all the way. Don't hold back anything.*

"As I stepped out into the aisle, an inspiration came. To symbolize my total commitment, I'd leave my watch, billfold, and car keys on the altar. This would say to the Lord that my time, treasures, and activities were at his call. Kneeling at the altar, I did just that—committed everything to God.

"Going back to my seat, I was shocked by my actions. They suddenly scared me. Had I gone off the deep end? What would happen now?"

John's fellow townspeople also were wondering. A few thought it was just a good show. Those who had watched John over the years knew that he was not to be taken lightly.

Home Headquarters

"Yes," says John, "if the Lord had wanted me to go into the pulpit ministry, I would have. Instead, he wanted me in ministry here in Woodland, heading up the furniture-manufacturing plant as I had been doing. It turned out as Paul says, 'Usually a person should keep on with the work he was doing when God called him'" (1 Corinthians 7:20, LB).

Then came John's arresting statement: "But, the ministry proved to be full-time: twenty-four hours a day—seven days a week—fifty-two weeks a year."

John's new dedication became evident in the plant, around town, and out into the state. Christian literature appeared in the plant's reception room and in John's office. As he does his daily errands around town, Christ and his church are often topics of discussion. His phones ring early and late, with calls from preachers and laypeople all over Georgia looking to John for guidance and leadership in setting up a mission weekend in their church or for some other church-related event. His responsibilities in the local church, the district, the South Georgia Conference, and the Georgia Episcopal Area comprise a staggering list.

"But," he quickly points out, "being a committed Christian involves more than being on church committees and filling one's off time with church activities. You can't really separate time for the Lord and time for business. They run together.

"For example, I may be sharing or witnessing about Jesus Christ to somebody in the plant, at my desk, on the phone, or on the street during so-called business hours. Or, when out on church work, I may be talking business or working out some deal. And, calls come in night and day for church, business, or both.

"When leaving those things at the altar, I had no idea of the beautiful way the Lord would make full use of my time, my area of operation, and my resources."

John reiterates, "After making my total commitment, the Lord kept me where I was, sending me to the places I knew and liked best—and he keeps me in all-the-time joyful ministry. It's thrilling to be able to share with my friends the wonderful things Jesus has done for me."

Bill Bassford, a lay leader in the First United Methodist Church in Valdosta, Georgia, where John coordinated a Lay Witness Mission, says of his ministry: "Our church will never again be the same. Neither will I. May the Lord keep him on the mission road."

John's experience makes the words of author Elton Trueblood come alive.

> The message is that the world is one, secular and sacred, and that the chief way to serve the Lord is in our daily work. The missionary task is not merely that of India and Africa, but that of America and Europe as well. The conversion of the world will not come by the efforts of clergymen merely, but by the efforts of all who are deeply committed. Thus there can be one central vocation, while there are many professions. Some persons can contribute most to the conversion of the world by working in banks, and some can do most by working in hospitals. We need guilds of devout politicians, guilds of devout lawyers, guilds of devout scholars.[1]

More World, Less Church

Sam Teague, a Tallahassee, Florida, banker and president of the $150,000,000 Sun Federal Savings & Loan Association, punctuates Trueblood's idea, "Christians need to spend more time witnessing in the world and less time in the church. The action today is in the world," he maintains, "not in the church."

Somewhat astounded, I challenged him to explain.

"First, Gus, I strongly support and am for the traditional church. My support is in the form of both time and money. But a lot of the church's witness is self-serving. While the church talks and ministers to itself, numerous people outside of it are searching frantically for fulfillment and purpose. Jesus Christ is their only answer, but most don't know it or can't find it. The only way they're going to hear about Christ is through Christians caring for them and sharing their experiences. In most cases, laypeople are the closest to these searchers and can help them the most.

"The practical result of this conviction is that my time in the church is limited so I can spend more time in the world."

"What do you mean specifically?" was my reaction.

"This," he replied. "I could spend most of my spare hours working on church committees and in church-related activities. These are good and necessary but not as important as getting the good news of Christianity into the world. Consequently, I limit my church time to teaching an adult class, participating in Sunday morning workship, plus a maximum of two Sunday speaking engagements per month in other churches.

"This opens up time for me to participate in business, community, and trade activities. In these are all kinds of opportunities for sharing Jesus Christ."

Pressed for a description of the kind of activities he participates in, Sam explained. "I have more calls for public service than time to perform them, so I pray for divine guidance to accept those with the greatest opportunities for

Christian witness. This has led me to such positions as being a member of the Tallahassee City Commission, serving twice as mayor, being a state senator, chairman of the Downtown Improvement Authority and a member of the Governor's Capitol Center Planning Commission, president of Florida Savings & Loan League, and director of Federal Home Loan Bank of Atlanta, the parent organization of 650 savings and loans in the Southeast. This leads to being on many committees within the savings and loan industry."

Sharing, Witnessing, Helping

"How do you witness in situations like those?" I queried.

"During my term as mayor in 1964, we were involved in the integration turmoil. When meetings got disruptive and nearly out of control, I'd sometimes say, 'Let's pause and ask Brother Jones to pray for our guidance.' Invariably, the meetings would then progress constructively.

"A more recent example was a meeting in Washington, D.C. We were embroiled in legislative proposals to be made and not getting anywhere. With a smile and a chuckle, I suggested, at the risk of being branded a fanatic, 'We're getting no place with our human wisdom. Why don't we try some supernatural wisdom?' As shock waves settled down, someone requested that I lead the group in a prayer. The meeting ended with some good positive results.

"Openly seeking God's guidance through prayer in public affairs is only one way to share our divine resources. Other ways that have come to me are references to appropriate scripture; the reflection of a positive, hopeful attitude that comes from a living, vital faith in God; and being concerned about people's needs. In addition, God is always opening up new and unexpected opportunities for sharing, witnessing, helping. For example, people frequently ask me where I get my optimism and how I cope with today's conditions. Many call me on the phone."

"How often do you receive calls?" I asked.

"It will average about two calls per day," Sam answered. "Among those, there's usually one during the week that opens up person-to-person sharing, even consulting. To be ready for this opportunity, I keep my calendar open every Monday from 11 A.M. to noon. This time is always used."

Curious as to the kind of situations that would cause Sam to set aside that one hour in the midst of a busy business week, I asked if he would share an example or two.

One concerned the president of a large manufacturing firm who wanted to know how he could get the peace and full confidence that he was in tune with God. Another concerned a young married woman whose husband had left her and their marriage was heading for a breakup.

Both situations had happy endings. Neither call came through the church but through Sam's contacts outside the church.

Magnetic Mirror

Sam's contention that Christians should spend more time witnessing in the world raised this question: "It's easy to see that someone like you, with great public exposure and concerns for people, could virtually give a witness just walking down the street. But what about the average person?"

Sam's quick answer: "Every true Christian has a concern and love for all people and particularly for those around whom he or she works and lives. That person's face and presence, reflecting joy, radiance, and the ability to deal with problems, will attract people to ask, sooner or later, what he or she has and how it can be obtained. But, to be useful in that way, one has to be sensitive and responsive to God's prompting at any hour of the day, any day of the week, and at any place. The Christian life should be so integrated with one's work, family, and recreation that positive, Christlike signals are being given at all times, both unconsciously and intentionally."

"Would you illustrate?" I asked.

"Yes," replied Sam. "If I'm in prayer and sensitive for this kind of experience, it will happen several times a week. Right now, one that comes to mind starts with a relatively young woman wandering into the class I was teaching one Sunday morning. She found a place in the back, sat alone, and got out before I could meet her. Next Sunday, I met her. During the worship service, my wife, Myra, and I sat in the back of the church. Sitting ahead of us two or three rows, I noticed the new woman and with her was a sandy-haired boy about ten years old. Going out we encountered them in the foyer. She introduced us to her son. Without advance thought, I asked if he liked to fish. He enthusiastically replied yes. Again, without premeditation, I asked, 'How would you like to go with me next Saturday?'

"Tears began to flow from his mother's eyes. Later I learned that she was divorced and had been praying for months that some man might come into her son's life, giving him companionship through hunting, fishing, and in other ways, so he could better develop a male image. My son had just gone off to college. I was lonely, and I liked to fish, so God also filled a need in my life.

"Over the past four years, this boy and I have developed our friendship, and he has grown into a fine young man. Had I not yielded to the impulse of inviting him to go fishing with me, both of us would have missed this rewarding experience."

I have known Sam for twenty-nine years, first as a businessman, then as a churchman, and finally as the complete success he has become. Over this time, I have been curious about the mystique that draws people to him, opening up their confidences, searchings, and needs any place and time. Then, too, there is his uncanny ability to come up with constructive, workable answers for difficult situations.

A Power Hour

This visit was my chance to put the question to him, "How do you account for this aura of yours that inaudibly says, There's hope—there's an answer—I'll help."

"First, Gus, I don't feel it's my aura. I pray that it might be God working through me. With all my heart, like committed Christians everywhere, I do want to be God's person where he has placed me and leads me.

"However, I have a routine that daily transforms me. It starts every morning after about six hours of sleep. Without an alarm clock, I automatically wake up between four-thirty and five. By six, I've had breakfast and am at a branch office.

"Roughly from six to seven, my time is devoted to Bible study, prayer, meditation, and preparation for teaching on Sunday. The heart of my prayer is to be open to what God has to say and to the ways in which he wants to use me during the day ahead.

"From seven to eight, I do the creative thinking that needs to be done. Even when traveling, this is the schedule I maintain so as not to break my living routine. By eight-thirty, if in Tallahassee, I arrive at our downtown office, empowered for the pressures of the day.

"The hour from six to seven gives me my power, direction, and readiness to respond to the calls of God during the demands of the day. It is such an exciting and vital encounter that I wake up eager for it."

I could now begin to understand Sam Teague and how he was able to develop the idea for attracting saving and loan deposits that then began to pour through the mail, filling several bushel baskets, getting Sun Federal off to a running start many years ago. It was easier to understand how the Lord gave him twenty minutes of supernatural inspiration for writing the outline of Wanted: Ten Brave Christians (also known as The Great Experiment).[2] From then, 1965, the disciplines of the Ten Brave Christians program have stirred the spirit for changing lives and renewing churches around the world. That early hour must provide Sam his relaxed presence, which charges a group of people with a desire to receive the power of God for their life. It also explains why Sam was so ready to board the plane early the following morning in Atlanta and to be at his downtown Tallahassee office near the usual time for opening.

Finally, it told me why Sam is on call by the Lord for service at any hour, at any place, often without notice, and why peace, purpose, and power are so evident in his life.

Points to Ponder

* Being a committed Christian includes putting all our time, talents, and treasures at God's disposal.
* When God calls, our starting point is usually where we are.
* Our witness and work for the Lord become integral parts of our secular responsibilities.
* Our contacts, work, and activities outside the church give us our greatest opportunities for sharing the good news.
* When the power and love of Christ in our lives is radiantly genuine, people seek to learn the source of our peace, power, and purpose.
* A regular time dedicated for daily prayer and Bible study, along with living constantly in a spirit of prayer, sensitizes us to the spiritual outcries and unrest of those around us.
* Sharing and caring come naturally for a committed Christian, confronting the searching and needs of the world.

CHAPTER 10

Step Out and Speak Up

*Let the redeemed of the Lord say so. (Psalm 107:2*a*)*

For if you tell others with your own mouth that Jesus is your Lord . . . you will be saved. (Romans 10:9, LB)

"Somewhere between seventy-five hundred and ten thousand people have watched me build sand castles along the shore of Myrtle Beach, South Carolina," estimates F. E. Hobeika of Dillon, South Carolina.

F.E. is an industrial mechanic at DuPont, and his sand castles are masterpieces of engineering and architecture. Built about six-feet square, two-feet high, and of different designs and complete with stairs, lookout towers, moats, and bridges, they have become almost as famous as Myrtle Beach itself and are viewed by people from all over the U.S. For fourteen years during his summer vacations, F.E. has been building replicas of noblemen's strongholds, devoting hard work five to eight hours a day, depending on the design. Over the last twelve years, he has been building one a day during his week at the beach, only to have each carefully detailed, sculptured creation washed away at night by the tide.

Castle Conversions

The *North Myrtle Beach Times* raised the question: "Why would a seemingly educated, well-spoken family man waste hours playing in the sand?"[1]

Hobeika's reply, "It's work for the Lord. The sand castles are merely symbols of life. Anyone's life that isn't built on the firm foundation of the Lord will crumble and wash away like a sand castle."

This self-taught sculptor relates that it started by entertaining his two daughters on the beach. The next year, the girls wanted more of the same. People had crowded around, when his daughter came calling him to dinner. Looking back, on the road to their cabin, he saw the crowd of fifty to sixty admiring his handiwork.

"In that moment," recalls F.E., "I saw how that castle could be used to illustrate what happens when a life is built without Jesus Christ. After dinner it was time to leave, but I vowed that if we ever got back, I'd use castles to witness."

Two years later, the family arranged another Myrtle Beach vacation. Remembering his vow, he tried out his object lesson. The crowds of interested people kept coming.

During a day, he figures that at least one hundred people come and go—sometimes more, sometimes less. They listen, ask questions, and respond to his unusual allegories. Some give enthusiastic encouragement, some pray, others offer to pass out tracts. Only one, over the years, has been verbally antagonistic.

Many have acknowledged Christ as their Savior as a result of this beautiful, fragile, and realistic illustration. F.E. receives cards and letters from all over the country. Many people return a second or third year to view and hear this unusual ministry. Some come to tell that, during the year, they became Christians because of his sand castle story.

From probing what background F.E. might have that would bring him to this experience comes this stimulating idea: "Sharing with people what Jesus does in your life is as natural as breathing or eating. When I have a new car, I like to tell others of its features. It's the same way with what Christ does for me. But we have to respond when Christ gives us our chance, or nothing happens. If I hadn't stepped out and done something about the idea the Lord gave me, I would have missed the joy of seeing scores of people who have been converted and those hundreds who cheer me on."

From Four Missions to Forty

Hearing of F.E.'s beach-side vision, my mind went back to a day in 1975. I was mowing our lawn, but all the time, subconsciously, my mind was lamenting the decline of Lay Witness Missions in Georgia. They had all but died out. Then came the thought: *Why not run advertisements in the* Wesleyan Christian Advocate *here in Georgia telling about Lay Witness Missions in other parts of the country.*

Suddenly, as though waking up, I realized the inward dialogue that was going on.

Lord, are you telling me something? I responded. *Should I do it?*

The answer I got was, "Talk to others—speak up about it." I did.

I was led to some fellow Georgians to whom the Lord also had spoken about the sharp decrease in missions. They agreed to share with me the cost of advertising. Inquiries for missions began to trickle in.

After five ads, run over a period of about two years and financially sponsored by sixteen men, the Georgia Laity Board of Renewal (GLBR) was organized. Its purpose was to bring together a group of laypeople who, on a sustained basis, would encourage more churches to hold Lay Witness events. In order to do so, these people made a commitment of money and time.[2] Their work is done in cooperation with the General Board of Discipleship of The United Methodist Church.

In 1977 the board scheduled four missions in Georgia. In 1978 GLBR started promoting missions. At the time of this writing, in 1981, there are roughly forty missions in Georgia. GLBR members say that an exciting result of this stepping out in faith is the great number of people finding new life in Christ and of churches that are being renewed. The GLBR is also encouraged by seeing similar programs, patterned after theirs, in several other states.

Five in One

Dr. Ken Chafin, speaking at the Robert H. Schuller Institute for Successful Church Leadership, tells of the results of another layperson, a woman, stepping out and speaking up.[3]

Dr. Chafin had just taken on the responsibilities of senior pastor at the large and rapidly growing South Main Baptist Church in Houston, Texas. He was feeling overwhelmed by the immensity of the task, when a woman came into his office with a declaratory question: "Are you aware that the level of Bible education in the seventeen Hispanic-speaking Baptist churches in our town is totally inadequate?"

Hesitatingly, Dr. Chafin conceded, only to be challenged by another question: "Do you feel it would be a good idea to do something about it?"

That brought up his defenses. He felt he was not properly doing what he had to do, let alone take on additional responsibilities.

She continued, "I wasn't asking you to do anything. I simply wanted to know if you were aware of the situation and if you felt it would be a good idea for some of us laypeople to tackle the problem?"

Dr. Chafin said, "Yes," and Mrs. Ruby Hill thanked him and walked out of the office. Some time later he was asked to review an expansive, carefully researched and organized program for selected laity to lead a program on Bible-teaching. It became known as the Leadership-Training Institute for the lay leaders of Hispanic Baptist churches in Houston.

Subsequent evaluation by an outside group revealed that, astoundingly, this program lifted the level of Bible knowledge in those Hispanic congregations to an equivalent of ten years of study in the typical church.

Ruby Hill, when questioned about this history-making

program, tended to describe it as a subprogram of previously begun ministries. Pressed to explain, she told of an effort that preceded the Institute, a weekday ministries program called SMILE (South Main's Informal Learning Experiences). It started with English classes for wives of international students and of employees in the Houston area, as well as for the Spanish-speaking people in the vicinity of the church. Then international clubs were organized that met weekly for children, mothers, and teen-agers.

This program expanded until, at one time, South Main had wives from twenty-nine different countries meeting on Tuesday mornings. The enthusiastic response from the foreign community led to their organizing a Sunday school department for internationals. Bible was taught to the adults in their own language, while the children went to regular English-speaking classes, as in the public schools.

Eventually, a full-time pastor to head up the work with internationals was added to the South Main staff. Today the church has four different ethnic minority congregations meeting in its facilities—Korean, Hispanic, Cambodian, and Chinese. The Chinese are moving out, setting up their own Houston Chinese Church with a beginning membership of over four hundred.

On Sunday, May 10, 1981, the following numbers of internationals attended worship at South Main:

Houston Chinese Church	543
South Main Hispanic Church	135
Korean Congregation	128
Cambodian Ministry	184

The weekly Tuesday morning gathering of international wives learning English was started in 1966 and currently has roughly one hundred forty enrolled. During the same period of time, South Main has grown to roughly seven thousand members.

Had Ruby Bauman Hill not listened to the Lord speaking

to her when she was a young lady of twenty-one living in Port Arthur, this story might never have happened. For some time, Ruby had realized that life could have a definite, divine purpose and direction, but these were missing in her life.

After discussion and prayer with her pastor, she made a commitment to God that she would be available for whatever he brought her way.

So, the Lord took charge. He started her teaching Sunday school, performing various jobs in the church, and led her two years later to a Christian marriage with Gordon Hill. They were blessed with a son. Her experience was broadened as the Hills moved from Port Arthur to Beaumont, then to Houston. Her work areas diversified from working with children to youth and then to women, preparing her for the big day.

People for Programs

Her moment came at age thirty-three. Attending a meeting of officers for the Texas Women's Missionary Union, she discovered with certainty her important calling. Sitting in this large audience of women from all over Texas, it seemed as though the speaker had singled her out in his message on the great need of missionary education and action. As though a picture had been flashed on a screen, in her mind she vividly saw the unique needs of her Houston community.

Even in that crowd, she felt alone—with God. Although not understanding how, she knew God was saying to her, "You are the person to fill the needs that you see." It was a sacred, moving experience, staying with her for life. That commitment between her and God was real and guided her to community service beyond her highest dreams.

"Following that encounter with God, things began to happen. I began to see more and more needs. Wonderful things came my way. My horizons expanded," Ruby told me.

"It was obvious that this was my unique area of work for him. The Lord brought special people into my life, having already begun with my husband and many others, especially Jane Robinson."

Jane was not only a member of the Sunday school class Ruby was teaching, she was also chairman of the Houston Baptist Mission Center board, devoted mostly to serving Spanish-speaking people. Ruby spoke out about the needs of the people in the vicinity of the church, many of whom were Spanish-speaking. Jane understood from firsthand experience. Together they started the SMILE program. Their husbands helped. Hundreds of volunteers now give of their time, energy, and money, with the church generously backing the whole program.

In retrospect, Ruby says, "I never could have done it alone. But when I spoke up about the needs God had shown me, he used my limited talents and the talents of friends and people I didn't know to work out the program and its details."

As a postscript she added, "I can't give you a story of dramatic physical experiences or of strange phenomena of God telling me what to do. My experience came in a very quiet, personal way, leaving a deep impression for the direction of my life. Then, as I stepped out and spoke up about what God had said to me, amazing, wonderful things began happening in my life."

Points to Ponder

* We often get directions from inner dialogue (subconscious prayer thinking) and sometimes from divine visions or from seeing a need growing out of experience.
* Our inner thoughts should surface in audible prayer for divine evaluation. This may lead us to human confirmation or rejection.
* To be used, we must be alert to his bidding.

* If we fail to respond to the inner voice, we lose the gift of divine hearing. It is enhanced by use.
* Our response to divine prompting often opens up privileges of service and commitment for others.
* Each person has a unique way of and circumstance for sharing.

CHAPTER 11

Risky Living

"I'm not asking you to take them out of the world, but to keep them safe from Satan's power." (John 17:15, LB)

*"Every one will be salted with fire." (Mark 9:49*b*)*

Following my return from World War II, I was in advertising a little over two years. Then in May 1948, I was appointed regional sales manager of a prefabricated-home manufacturing company. My region was Wisconsin and northern Illinois. This chapter picks up in November 1950.

Wednesday morning I was at breakfast in Chicago with the general manager and with the president and owner. The manager came to the point.

"We're thinking of opening a southern division with headquarters at Jackson, Mississippi. We already have a plant and plant manager not far from Jackson. We're wondering if you might be interested in being our southern division sales manager and opening up the territory. As such, you would become vice-president of the company."

The offer dazed me. This step up the ladder appealed to my thirty-six-year-old ambitions. On the other hand, we had good business going in Wisconsin, annually shipping in about one hundred fifty homes. Our little Mequon Community Methodist Church had been recently organized, and we had just completed building it. I was chairman of the board. Estelle was the Sunday school superintendent. And there was Hidden Acres, our subdivision, almost sold out. We were getting established.

Estelle's reaction was, "Oh, no. I just came home from buying all new wallpaper for the living and dining rooms. But," she added, "whatever you feel is the right thing to do, I'm with you."

Way to the World

Answers to our prayers seemed to say, "You'll be getting deeper into the world. Isn't that your calling?"

Building from scratch a sales and distribution organization in a territory from Texas and Arkansas to Maryland and everything south was a great challenge.

In early December, sitting across the desk from the general manager at the main headquarters, I gave him the word that we gladly would take the offer.

As he outlined my responsibilities, there was one mandate: "You must market the same, regular line of homes in the South as we do in the North."

Realizing the efficiencies in the administration, engineering, and production of standardized design, I quickly agreed. I reasoned that the price advantages of prefabricated production would offset any design differences of the North as compared with the South.

February 1, 1951, with a signed contract, I boarded a plane for Jackson. It was my first look at the market. In June, the family followed—Estelle, Greg (7), Gwen (4½), Gerrit (3). A new life ahead.

With our straight commission terms, finding and signing up good salespeople was easy. We soon had men placed in Texas, Louisiana, Mississippi, Alabama, Florida, Kentucky, and Washington, D.C. Field reports were optimistic. My production projections excited everybody.

The general manager, elated with our start, was very encouraging. His letter of commendation, received after our first sales meeting, gave me a lift that lasted throughout my sales management career.

Orders for model homes began to come in. We were grateful for every order, but the production people at the plant wished they would come in faster. The assembly line was set up for building a home an hour. Our sales reply was, "When we have our model home promotions, you'll see volume."

Builders put on good shows. Most were modeled after the Jackson program, in which a leading realtor excited the market by featuring the economy and quality of factory-built housing. People lined up for two blocks to see the new idea in housing, but out of the crowd of thousands, he only sold one home. Other open-house promotions had similar results, although most were not as dismal.

Reports began to come in, "People don't like the design." Then, as the capable, straight-commission factory representatives began to realize that their six-months' effort and expense could go down the drain, the reports came in like thunder.

Southern Problems

I headed to the field to check out the situation. Builders had invested thousands to attract crowds, and competitively, we had a bargain. But aesthetically, according to southern standards, we were out of it. Only a few people bought our homes. We were not getting the sales volume necessary to generate mass production.

I sounded out main headquarters about the problem. The response was, "Sell what you have."

We pushed on and came up with new marketing strategies. The field tried again, but results were limited. Sales representatives' money began to run out. One or two quit. Others were threatening to do the same unless we quickly came up with different designs.

Main headquarter's advice: "If a representative stumbles

and falls, pick up his sales catalog and give it to another." We did.

Eventually, almost too late, my dilemma came into clear focus. The realization haunted my mind: *The heavy investment of the company and the representatives is about to be washed out. Management insists on selling what we have. It sounds like they would close down the southern division before they would change designs. When I took the job, I agreed to market the regular line. Am I letting down the company? What about the representatives who have spent their savings—like the one who put a second mortgage on his home—and cannot make it? Am I failing both the company and the reps? What can I do? What should I do?*

Frustrated and not knowing which way to turn, Estelle and I prayed: "Lord, we want to do the right thing. We want to fulfill our commitment to the company. We also want to be true to you. If there is a sales idea that Gus has overlooked, show him. If this is the time for Gus to side with the field, give him the wisdom and strength to do so. And, Lord, you know we have a family to look after, four children now, since Gail has arrived. We really need you. Amen."

After some desperate cries of "save me" and more pressure from the field, plus my being helpless to do anything more, this positive, action answer emerged in my mind: *If something isn't done soon, everybody in the South—division and reps alike—will be going under. My commitment to help make the division successful should be greater than my commitment to design. To advocate changing the design would be in contradiction with company policy. It could mean dismissal for me. I'll risk it.*

Our prayer of thanks and petition was: "Thank you, Lord, for showing us the right thing to do. Now give Gus the wisdom and courage to make the presentation. And, Lord, if this means losing his job, we put our family in your hands. We have no other way to turn. Help us, and we know you will, whatever. Thank you. We love you. We trust you. Amen."

Facing the Facts

A board meeting was called for Monday morning, ten o'clock. Our southern plant manager and I picked up our airline tickets. He supported my position.

Armed with sales results and testimonials from the field, I went to urge a southern line of homes. All kinds of evidence showed that our marketing strategy, quality, and price were outstanding. My conclusion was that the design was out of sync with southern life-styles.

Based on prayer, research, and Estelle's unwavering support, I went into the meeting with conviction and courage. Sides shortly became evident. Two of the top officers stood firm, insisting on no change. The southern plant manager and I advocated the absolute necessity of new design. A famous home designer promised a limited new line in thirty days if the board wanted it. The president listened. Others were noncommital.

Monday night about eight, the meeting adjourned with no decision. We would reconvene at nine Tuesday morning.

My prayer that night was: *Thank you, Lord, for helping me make a strong case for what you showed me to do. A decision hasn't been given, but it seems I've done right by you. For Estelle, me, and our family, we know this means that all things work together for good to them that love God, to them who are the called according to his purpose—whatever the outcome may be. Thank you for this assurance. Amen.*

Tuesday noon the board adjourned for the executive committee to meet. The wait at the hotel for the results dragged on till about nine in the evening when the president called.

"Gus, you'll have a line of southern homes." Then he added, "From now on, you'll be reporting to me because our general manager is leaving the company."

The new line of homes saved the southern division. After a period of time, the plant was profitably producing an average of more than twenty homes per week and ready for more.

I prayed: *Thank you, Lord, for wisdom to understand the crisis. I'm grateful for Estelle's faith and support and for your hearing our prayers. Help me now to expand the business you've given us and to be a good representative of yours in all that I do.*

Word got around about the beautiful line of southern homes and about the southern operation. We shipped homes by train to Washington, D.C., Virginia, and Maryland and by trucks to shorter distances. Then, one day we got a call about our interest in shipping a thousand or more homes to European military sites for NATO housing.

The company nominated me to head up this program. We brought together a contractor capable of multimillion-dollar bonding, a consortium of banks in this country and in France for furnishing construction financing, and sources for long-term financing.

Arrangements were completed. The deal was ready. The date for starting shipments was soon. And then—it fell through.

I forgot the deal and went on to other things. One associate didn't give up easily. About six months later, he called me at our Jackson office. He had a new approach to the overseas housing, less exposed to foreign competition. He felt that he, another man, and I could wrap up the deal. Was I interested, and would I come to New York and help? I said yes.

Since this meeting was so crucial, he wanted no distractions and an atmosphere for creative thinking. He invited us to his and his wife's lovely home.

A few words about my associate. In many ways, he was a business-world ideal of mine. He was gracious and possessed know-how. He was somebody special to me.

Two-sided Coins

The evening started with opening the bar and pouring the drinks. Their surprise was very evident as I requested ginger ale.

A threatening inner voice said, *You're insulting his hospitality. You may lose their confidence. You look like a square. You might kill the deal for your company.*

A positive thought followed. *It would be wrong to compromise your commitment in order to get the business. Stand firm. Try all the harder to make the program work.*

"How come you don't drink, Gus?" they asked.

In response, I simply shared my background and Christian convictions. They accepted me for what I was.

Despite my initial feelings of self-doubt, plans progressed constructively. Finally, complications with the international commodities market and the state department kept the program from being accepted. However, our business friendship and appreciation continued to grow. Our mutual respect lasted over the years.

Now, as I read Lloyd Ogilvie, I can understand his statement: "Unless there is some area of resistance to what we believe and are doing in obedience to Christ, there may be some question about how much we believe. . . . Often our troubles come from the intersection of our faithfulness to Christ and the values and standards of our culture."[1]

This statement, along with other reflections, leaves me somewhat chagrined at the length of time it took me to resolve the defensive feelings about my so-called straight living in worldly situations. The latter seem to go with lots of travel, public relations, hard selling, and army life.

For a long time the question had lingered in my mind whether it was an illusion or fact that success of a particular deal was linked to being "one of them," to getting in with the people with whom I was dealing. The old cliché "When in Rome, do as the Romans" was a powerful temptation.

So, when turning down invitations or encouragement to participate in intrigue, gambling, sex, drinking, padded expense accounts, under-the-table payoffs, personal side deals, using company time for personal purposes—and one of the toughest—keeping God as top priority, plus other things, I felt like an oddball and inwardly often feared rejection and loss of business, even opportunities.

Then, too, there was the other side of the coin, which could give the impression of being "holier than thou." That attitude, in some respects, I learned, is as bad as participation in things in which you do not believe.

Some of my dear Christian friends asked, and others wondered, "Why put up with it, Gus? Why not get into some line of work where you don't have to face uneasiness along with the encouragement and danger of compromising your principles?"

Temptation and Trust

My answer was not every Christian's answer. But it gave me harmony with God. The answer went back to that muddy dip in the lane—God's call meant to me: "Do not try to run away or to escape or to hide out from the world. Instead, meet temptations head on. I will help you to overcome, and in so doing, I will use you for my purposes."

From this concept, it became my conviction that God was saying to me, "Be my man in the world. When you are faced with temptations, trust me. Risk failure to live for me. Love the people who are different and who tempt you but don't be a part of their wrongdoing. I'll see you through."

This put me in many unsavory and seemingly untenable situations. The Lord did help me to love people with different ideas, even opposite life-styles, as compared with mine. My discovery was that love and appreciation are stronger than differences. My ability to affirm people turned out to be a business asset.

Undoubtedly, my offbeat business life-style cost me some short-term advantages, including some deals. However, in the long run, as short-term operators fouled up or dropped out, it gave me some of my greatest opportunities.

Finally, out of many different experiences came the conclusion: The Christian life-style is a success life-style.

Some illustrations may help explain.

We had spent considerable time putting together a program of a hundred or more homes, with the promise of many more to follow. I was advised that the principal involved wanted our homes. He liked our program. When could we start shipping? Then, aside, very discreetly, a third party told me that the way to glue the arrangements together and to keep out competition was to include a modest figure of compensation for the government man involved. The party made it clear that it was not a demand but would ensure our success. My response was that we did not operate that way, and I proposed that we rest our case on its merit. Although everything was supposed to have been ready to ship, we never received the signed orders for starting.

Months after the negotiations, blazing headlines told of the indictment of a prominent FHA man for accepting bribery. He was the one who liked our homes, wanted our program, and whom we were supposed to have paid. We lost the order but chalked up a victory in not being trapped in illegal dealing.

Monday Morning Miracle

One event after another could be recalled concerning the way God helped our family to turn problems in our new business into great possibilities. One of the most interesting is the case of Imperial Homes' first engineer (after I served with the aforementioned company for 9 years and with Kingsberry Homes for 3½, Estelle and I organized Imperial Homes, another home-manufacturing company).

This engineer was basically a good draftsman. As our business grew, we needed someone who had a deeper understanding of housing design and structural engineering. Our first man was faithful, and we did not feel like letting him go. We also concluded that we could not afford two engineers for the amount of business we were doing at the time. We were praying about an answer.

Estelle, Gerrit, Gail, and I took off for a weekend at Lake Junaluska, North Carolina. Gwen, our oldest daughter, stayed home to keep the office open Saturday morning. Shortly before noon I was called to the phone. It was Gwen, saying the Imperial engineer had another job and had to report Monday morning.

Fine, except we had a fairly heavy production schedule and no one else to do the preparatory engineering. Estelle and I prayed for a Monday morning answer. The best we had as we drove back Sunday afternoon was to make a call or two on some possible prospects, but we kept praying.

Monday morning, just after I turned on the lights in my office and pulled out my notes for the day, my secretary called to say there was a man to see me.

The man turned out to be Milt Bolkcom, a Southern Tech valedictorian graduate in light construction engineering. He had enough experience in our field to have earned the reputation of being one of the bright, young engineers in home manufacturing. I already knew about his background, so by nine o'clock that Monday morning, we had our new engineer. He was capable of growth with the company and had the ability to train others. Truly he was the answer to our prayers.

Reserves for Risk

Finally, an observation came to me that took much of the anxiety and fear out of risk-taking. It is easy to see in the experience of a dear friend, Ralph Freeman.

We attended a Methodist Men's retreat at Pine Mountain, Georgia. The backdrop of mountains was covered with breathtaking, vivid red, yellow, and bronze leaves. We were only a short distance from FDR's hideaway White House. Ralph, twenty-three, led the singing, and I led the retreat.

As he prepared to leave early, we discovered that he was going to a renewal audition for singing with the Atlanta Symphony. We paused to pray for his success. That audition was another success in a series of continuing ones for Ralph. It led to his being called to sing across America and in foreign lands to audiences of thousands.

The miracle of Ralph is that he has had virtually no professional voice training. His musical training in high school and college was with instruments. His college major was in mathematics and physics. With an outstanding college record, he was picked up quickly by IBM. Starting as a marketing man with IBM office systems, he later was promoted to corporate college relations and recruiting in the Southeast. He was then selected to be one of the few specialized marketing representatives in IBM's new field of bio-medical systems.

As he spiraled upward in IBM, he received more and more calls for his singing. Something unexpected was happening to him.

As he memorized, practiced, and sang spiritual songs, he felt a closeness and awareness of God in his life. This moved him emotionally. As he sang, inspired by the Holy Spirit, he was overcome by the presence of God and became almost oblivious of his audience. Some people described it as "singing his heart out." When he found that an audience was having a listening experience very similar to his singing experience, this gave him a lift that stayed with him.

The pull on his life to do more singing grew stronger and stronger. There were suggestions of devoting his life to the ministry of singing. But, he had a problem. As a singer, he couldn't match his rocketing income. He prayed for divine guidance.

Out of it came this life-releasing insight, "And with all his abundant wealth through Christ Jesus, my God will supply all your needs" (Philippians 4:19, GNB).

Thinking about the responsibility of providing for his wife, Elaine, and their four children, ages three to ten, he talked to IBM about his problem. They offered him a year's leave of absence without pay so he could see what would happen when he spent full time singing.

Shortly before the end of that year, he took this message to his friends at IBM, "Thank you, but I shall not be returning. On November 14, 1980, in the Civic Center in Atlanta, I will make my national debut as a professional singer."

Ralph shares that he got the nerve to take that leap in faith because he was able to put his complete trust in God as the supplier of all his needs.

Now, six months after terminating with IBM, Ralph acknowledges that income has not equaled what it was before and living adjustments have had to be made.

Then he adds. "I have no worry. Fulfilling God's call for my life, I know he is going to care for me and my family. Operating in his will, he gives me answers and direction that I need. This faith and knowledge give me a freedom and joy for living such as I've never before experienced."

"Doesn't your banker," I asked, "think it's pretty risky for you, at thirty-three with a family of six, to launch a career in an entirely different field when you were doing so well in your business and the sky was the limit?"

With a seriousness and conviction that amplified this assuring answer to his risk, Ralph replied, "Yes, he does, but what he does not understand is that I have an underwriter for all my risks and the world's greatest booking agent. That's Jesus Christ."

Points to Ponder

* Putting Jesus Christ first over occupational temptations involves risk of failure.
* Living in the world, we must be prepared to risk failure and rejection in living out our commitment for Jesus Christ.
* Losses because of Christian principles often make us winners.
* We frequently win by risking principle over wrong practice.

* Keeping God as top priority in our lives generates motivation, a sense of freedom, courage, and creativity, whereas compromise with wrongdoing causes uneasiness, guilt, defensiveness, and, eventually, paralysis of the possibilities for effective accomplishment.
* A Christian has resources for turning problems into possibilities.
* A stance of honesty, dependability, know-how, and appreciation of others' qualities give stronger personal and public relations support than adjusting to habits of social compatibility.
* A Christian life-style develops qualities for long-term success.

EXPERIENCE IV

God Gives Victory

Hearing and responding to God's call are only the first steps in God's unfolding future for the committed.

Once we step out to serve, we find he guides us into strange and unexpected areas of preparation.

When the battles of principalities and powers would destroy the thing to which we have given our lives, we suddenly discover a power beyond ourselves.

With steadfast faith, the promised victory becomes a reality for now and for the future, in this life and in the life beyond. We make the thrilling discovery of seeing God's call come to full bloom. To our surprise, it is more exciting and beautiful than we ever foresaw or dared to dream—and this is just the beginning for the called.

CHAPTER 12

Power for the Call

*I pray that you will begin to understand how incredibly great his power is to help those who believe him. (Ephesians 1:19*a*, LB)*

Now glory be to God who by his mighty power at work within us is able to do far more than we would ever dare to ask or even dream of—infinitely beyond our highest prayers, desires, thoughts, or hopes. (Ephesians 3:20, LB)

"J.P. would run me ragged. At that time he was around sixty, and I was right at forty. I'd get six to seven hours of sleep a night, while J.P. would get four or five. Staying in his home and working with him during the day, I saw firsthand what people had told me. Even then it was hard to believe. This was J. P. Stafford's pace for over twenty years. It was absolutely astonishing to see his stamina and unlimited source of energy."

These words of Judge Robert Mayfield, Lebanon, Missouri, describe the reputation of the six-foot-three-inch, relaxed, deep-voiced, chuckling, Mississippi planter and inspired Methodist lay leader, known across U.S. Methodism simply as J.P.

Judge Mayfield went on to describe his travels with J.P. "I'd get up about six-thirty to be ready for breakfast at seven. Meeting J.P. then, I learned that he had been up at least two hours, sometimes longer. He had started his men and tractors in the fields, and the daily farm work was planned and scheduled. After breakfast, he attended to other chores. By ten or eleven, we would leave for one of the districts of the Mississippi Conference, of which he was the lay leader. Preceding interstates, the conference had an almost two-hundred-mile diameter of two-lane highways. J.P. lived at the far northwest corner.

"By 9 P.M., the meetings were usually over, and we would start back to Cary with a two- to four-hour ride ahead of us, depending on where we were.

"Getting home anywhere from eleven to one, we would catch some sleep and start the next day on the same schedule, until we had covered all the districts in his conference. If J.P. wasn't busy in Mississippi, he was busy somewhere else in the U.S., on a similar schedule, helping build The Methodist Church."

"And, what happened?" I asked the judge, who from his twenty years of heading lay activities was able to watch and evaluate J.P.'s work in the church.

"His conference," replied Mayfield, "led the nation in the number of Methodist Men's groups chartered by the national office. He was a pacesetter. Methodist Men would not be on the level it is today if it had not been for Stafford and a few other men of whom he was the leader.

"He was one of the chief architects of the commission form of organization in the local church under which we operate today. This concept came out of the legislative committee and was adopted by the 1964 General Conference.

"The Purdue National Congress of Methodist Men is another major quadrennial event of the general church that carries the imprint of his organizational design. He was one of the organizers of the first congress held in 1954. His influence was felt on both the general planning and program committees. As you might expect, his conference was one of the largest in attendance.

"Then, too, he was a member of the General Coordinating Council, which regulated all the general boards of the church, and was the forerunner of today's General Council on Ministries.

Divine Drive

Reflecting on this man's tremendous list of accomplishments during the years of retirement for most people, I asked Bob, "What was the source of his strength and drive?"

After thinking awhile, Bob replied, "Of course, J.P. was inspired. He felt divinely called. He was always pumping adrenalin at a high rate. But he did one thing I've never seen so clearly. He literally prayed at all times. As we were traveling, discussing some challenge, he would often say, 'Let's pray'—as many as four or five times in a working day. In my opinion, that was the main source of the high level of zest and enthusiasm for his life's mission."

J.P.'s answer to the question was a little different. Putting the two answers together, we get an insight on developing power for living.

"There were times when I'd feel tired," said J.P. "But, I discovered that concentrating on opportunities to be captured would give me energy—like an athlete in training: The more I do, the more power I develop. The body has a way of accommodating to challenges. Also, Paul's advice greaty influenced me. I learned its value from experience: 'Be joyful always, pray at all times, be thankful in all circumstances' (1 Thessalonians 5:16-18*a,* TEV).

"Meditating and praying constantly, I received guidance on how to do things and, also, was shown the far-reaching possibilities of new things to be done. Steadily operating in that manner, it becomes understandable, as Bob says, that adrenalin runs high. You get excited and feel good about what you're doing. You don't want to stop at the end of the day, and you want to get going in the morning. I've observed over the years that when God gives you a call, he also gives you power to carry it out."

Called to Build

A resounding southern Baptist amen to J.P.'s discovery comes from Wallace Johnson, whose early call to be a builder led him to becoming one of today's towering, inspiring men of our nation.

My first contact with Wallace was in the sixties, in the National Association of Home Builders. Previous reading of trade-news releases had informed me of his historic home-building programs for blacks in the late forties and early fifties. Also, his spectacular increase in new home starts during the war put him in the national spotlight. While working with him on committees, it was easy to see there was something special about this man. What I discovered and saw was only the beginning of his contribution to the history of our land.

Born into the humble surroundings of a Mississippi sharecropper family that was short on cash but long on faith, Wallace feels that from the day of his birth he was destined to be a carpenter and contractor. With deep conviction he adds, "I believe I have been called to build just as surely as preachers have been called to preach."[1] The living story of his fantastic life gives credence to his claim. It is the story of a strong faith that overshadows the hardships under which he grew up and the pitfalls of the business climate in which he operated.

At thirty-eight he discovered how to generate power for accomplishment. This changed his life from one of existence living to one of continuous unfolding fulfillment, opportunities, and success. He was a building supplies salesman making $37.50 a week. He was having a hard time making a go of it and was deeply frustrated. The dramatic turning point of his life is shared by him.

"Although I went to church and believed in God, somehow I had disassociated my job from my religion. One night I made my prayer more specific:

"Lord, I've been trying to make a go of it as a salesman,

but I'm not doing very well. What am I doing wrong? Show me, Lord, the direction I should go, the people I should see, the way I should use my time.

"From the moment I stopped trying to accomplish everything with my own resources and prayed to God for guidance, things were different. Names of people to see, places to go, popped into my mind. Where did these suggestions come from but from God? Ideas certainly hadn't flooded my mind before I asked him for help."[2]

By the end of that year, 1939, backed by their pastor's prayer for blessing and direction, Wallace and Alma, his wife, went into business on their own. In 1940, they built 181 homes. During 1941 they won recognition building a house a day. By 1945 they were one of the nation's top builders, building 3,000 homes—1,000 more than their goal.

People who know about the building business recognize the fantastic feat of going from zero to 3,000 homes during the brief span of six years. The Johnsons accomplished this during 1940–45, World War II years. Materials, if available, were on allocation. Most construction men were fighting the war or building planes. Money was being directed to the production of materials essential to victory. The market was fragmented, with young fathers being drafted and with families doubling up for the duration.

"How did they do it?" ask builders, finance men, salespeople, and others who understand construction and the times. Wallace answers by revealing the secret of their buoyancy, facing these seeming impossibilities.

"I made lists of our needs and problems and prayed over them. When desperate for lumber, I asked the Lord to guide me to it. When I needed men, I asked Him to help me find them. When I needed loans, I asked Him to send me to the right bankers. And He did."[3]

Answers to Wallace's prayer lists constitute a book in themselves. One typical illustration tells the story of the Johnsons' power in overcoming obstacles.

One day Wallace's prayer list contained the notation

"Show me where to get lumber." In a rush, he took a country shortcut and got lost. Coming upon a sawmill with lots of stacked lumber and beautiful standing timber nearby, he almost feared it was a mirage. Picking up two boys looking for a ride, Wallace asked what they knew about the mill. He learned it was for sale. Twenty-four hours later he was the owner of a million feet of lumber, mules, and some standing timber.

The prayer list became life's anchor for the Johnsons' stormy days. They prayed together at their morning breakfast devotion. Wallace carried the list with him and prayed throughout each day. The lists came to be more than lists of petition. They also became lists of vision as God planted ideas in the minds of these committed builders.

Thus as Wallace traveled, he observed the plight of black housing. That need went on his list. It became his new vision. The answer to that prayer was God's example for the nation of how the need for new homes for blacks could be provided. Wallace's prayer for having a constructive, out-reaching, open-minded attitude proved to be the gateway to many opportunities.

The most amazing of these came as he answered the phone one night, while doing his work for the next day. He had more work than could be finished that night, and the caller wanted to see him right away. His openness to new ideas overrode the demands of his unfinished papers of figures and plans and the deep sigh of an already full day. He responded, "Yes, come on over."

By 2 A.M., he had caught the vision with Kemmons Wilson of a national chain of family motels. The name of the chain, confirmed that night in 1953, was Holiday Inn.

When Wallace retired in 1976 on his seventy-fifth birthday, there were "1,700 Holiday Inns in operation with more than 278,000 rooms. According to an *Institutions* magazine survey, the Holiday Inns system provides more food and lodging than any other group in the world—except the United States Army!"[4]

Wallace's prayer list and living prayer made a game out of the challenges and demands of his busy life. He even regards his work as fun. Before retirement, this enjoyment centered around being vice-chairman of the board of Holiday Inns, chairman of the board of three major corporations, each doing business in the millions, vice-president of a fifth major company, and officer in seventy other corporations.

You're It!

After retirement, he began to unload responsibilities. But while simplifying his life, he became a committee member of Campus Crusade for Christ International. The committee's task was to find an international chairman for the new crusade to be known as Here's Life. Wallace was challenged by the crusade's objectives.

> It would take the good news of Jesus Christ and the Gospel to every nation on earth! It would fulfill the great commission in this generation! . . . the vision . . . could change the world from one of violence, crime, immorality, racial unrest and bitterness, jealousy and materialism to the world of peace, beauty, and brotherhood that God intended it to be.[5]

This must be the vision of the future chairperson, who must understand international relations and how to raise millions of dollars needed to get this globe-encircling job done.

Other members of this search committee were Dr. Bill Bright, president of Campus Crusade for Christ International, San Bernardino, California; Dr. Joe L Mayes, president of Mayes International, Dallas, Texas; Nelson Bunker Hunt, chairman of Hunt Energy Corporation, Dallas, Texas; Roy Rogers and Dale Evans, entertainers, Victorville, California; and Jim McKinney and Doug Dillard, representing Campus Crusade.

Wallace invited them to breakfast in Memphis for their first meeting to consider candidates for this awesome responsibility. Bill Bright, presiding, started the meeting by announcing that a precommittee meeting had been held and a decision made. Wallace was taken aback with this news and a bit miffed for having been left out. Trying not to show his hurt, he said, "You mean to tell me you've already made the selection?"

Bright said, "'Yes,' and then pointed his finger at me: 'And that man is *you*.'"[6]

After feeble attempts at declining and after recovering from the shock, the invitation went onto his prayer list. He consulted with friends. The confirmation was unmistakably a call from God for him to accept. On April 22, 1977, at age seventy-six, he wrote his letter of acceptance to Bill Bright.

Reflecting on this new call in his life, Wallace comments, "I am convinced that all that went before was just God's way of preparing me for the great task I now have undertaken."[7]

Talking with Brother Wallace on the phone June 23, 1981, he told me that $250,000,000 had been raised for Here's Life.

Wallace Johnson's enthusiasm is still ringing as he approaches eighty. He says, "The Lord has blessed us miraculously. It is the greatest privilege of my life to share with the world my discovery of the source of power to fulfill his call—prayer in the name of Jesus Christ!"

Points to Ponder

* Constant prayer gives energy and vision for new challenges.
* Seeing godly leadership come alive in other people as a result of answering God's call is so exciting it causes the called to start the day earlier and work later.
* Tentmaking, self-support, while serving the Lord, as with Paul, is the foundation for much inspired Christian leadership today.
* A daily written prayer list, developed in concert with God's will, produces power for and progress in fulfilling God's call.

* Problems diminish when we take them to God.
* As prayers are answered, God provides new openings and responsibilities, greater than ever before.
* Prayer for being open to God's ideas brings great and unexpected opportunities.

CHAPTER 13

Born to Win

*"Nobody has left home or brothers or sisters or mother or father or children or land for my sake and the gospel's without getting back a hundred times over, now in this present life, homes and brothers and sisters, mothers and children and land—though not without persecution." (Mark 10:29-30*a, *Phillips)*

The pivotal time in Jimmy Stallings' life was the summer of '71. He was living with the guilt complex of slipping out whenever he could for beer drinking, not approved by Louise, his wife. Also, for one to two hours on Sunday mornings, he would put on his Christian attire, then leave it in the closet the rest of the week. Of course, he saw to it that he was a relatively good giver to the First United Methodist Church of Stanton, Texas, and he served in official capacities and was regarded as a good churchman. But, Jimmy knew better.

Family Changes

Twila, their oldest daughter, then fifteen, had been causing the Stallings some deep concerns. But she went to a youth revival in July and came back a new person. The change was so dramatic and beautiful that it got to Jimmy. He saw how love replaced her rebellion and appreciation took the place of defiance. This marked change made him think of his own double standard of living. It began to bother him.

"Just a few days after Twila's change, while I was in New York," relates Jimmy, "I saw something that added to my uneasiness. It was a wino aimlessly shuffling along the street, from one side to the other. He was a picture of hopelessness and ruin. But what really got to me about that abject character was the supply of beer cans stuffed in every pocket. They seemed to taunt my desire for beer drinking. That pitiful picture would not be pushed out of my mind.

"Back home, within the week, the youth led the evening worship service in our church. Twila was part of it. The youngsters told about the excitement of having Christ in their lives, about the purpose of living that he gave them. Their lively singing reflected their joy. Seeing and hearing these young people tell of their faith was infectious.

"Yes, Gus, it looked like every way I turned during that month of July, the Lord was talking to me, pouring it on."

The climax was the district superintendent's speaking in their church Sunday evening, August 1.

"Everything the district superintendent said sounded like he was talking directly to me, stepping on my toes," explains Jimmy, and continues, "but when I understood what he was saying, I could see a way of unloading my guilt and substandard and double standard of living. No revival chorus had ever touched me like the one that night. It rang in my ears.

I surrender all, I surrender all,
All to Thee, my blessed Saviour, I surrender all.

"Then came the verse that voiced my inmost prayer.

All to Jesus I surrender, Humbly at His feet I bow,
Worldly pleasures all forsaken, Take me, Jesus, take me now.

"That hymn tugged at my heart, prodding me to step out and go to the altar, but strangely, my being was frozen. I could not move. Instead, from the time of that chorus's pull until I got home, something was saying to me, 'Tell Louise.'

"After we got in that night, I finally got up my nerve and blurted out to her, 'Louise, with the help of God, I'm going to turn my life around. You know what I mean. It means a different life-style for me. I'm sorry for the worries I have caused you.'

"Then I shared with my pastor, neighbors, and friends. After repenting of it all, I felt clean and free. I know from experience what Christ meant when he said, 'You will know the truth, and the truth will set you free' (John 8:32, GNB)."

This conversion experience became the footing of faith that led to the happy ending of the following painful story.

In the mid '70s, Jimmy and Louise's youngest daughter, Susan, moving into her upper teens, began experimenting with drugs. Gradually, she became hooked. She took harder and harder drugs until she became addicted to heroin. Supporting her habit led to all kinds of irregularities, including dropping out of college, writing bad checks, and becoming completely estranged from home, so that the Stallings did not know where she was.

Listening, Lord

Jimmy describes his and Louise's reaction as parents. "The situation was bad. We could not communicate with her, did not know what to do, were not able to handle it. It just killed us."

They tried one thing and another, proposing psychiatrists, lawyers, counselors, other services, only to be rebuffed by Susan. The situation continued to deteriorate. They offered to take care of her bad checks if she would go for professional help and treatment. That did not work.

"At the end of our rope, having had to disassociate ourselves from Susan," explains Jimmy, "and having tried to work it out in our way and with our strength, we started listening to God instead of asking him to listen to us."

Dejected, defeated, not talking, not knowing what to say, Jimmy and Louise sat at the kitchen table. She noticed *The*

Upper Room devotional guide, picked it up, and abstractedly started thumbing through it. She spotted the notice: "Do you need prayer? Call The Upper Room Living Prayer Center, 1-615-327-HOPE."[1]

"Why not try it?" Louise asked.

"I'd be willing," replied Jimmy. "It's for sure we haven't been able to do it ourselves."

They placed the call, and by the providence of God, Jimmy feels, Mary Etta Duffey was the prayer center volunteer.

Louise describes, "She seemed to know just what to say. Instantly, we related. She listened, accepted us, and held out hope—our trusting in God. Her beautiful prayer put us in touch with God."

After hanging up the phone and praying, they seemed to get what appeared to be an utterly impossible direction: Commit Susan to a state hospital.

First, they did not know where Susan was, but they thought she was somewhere in Lubbock. By now, she was of age, and they remembered again the bitter disappointments of her previous stony resistance to any positive help. Moreover, a court order would be required. Remembering Mary Etta's advice of trusting God, their hope was revived, and they prayed once more. "Lord, if that's what you're saying, we'll try again. We know that the only way this effort can succeed is by your supernatural intervention. We want to move in your will and be led by you. Be with us, we pray."

Those one hundred plus Texas miles between Stanton and Lubbock had never seemed so long as on that fateful Friday morning.

In Lubbock, they began to look for clues of her whereabouts and were tipped off that she was living in a house with several others. Before confronting her, they went to court to get the order. Almost as expected, the instructions were "You'll have to get your daughter to come in and be examined by a psychiatrist who will recommend commitment."

Jimmy's first reaction: "Impossible. How can we do that? She won't even talk to us. But we'll try again."

The Lord Leads

The tip proved to be right.

"And the Lord prepared the way," Jimmy acknowledges. "The night before, she had gotten into a bad row with another girl and had her face beaten, leaving a broken nose. Susan needed hospital treatment and was ready for it. Once in the hospital, we got her into the psychiatric ward. Then we got the court order."

Again, by the grace of God, explains Jimmy, the court assigned a compassionate attorney to Susan. In an understanding manner, he persuaded her to sign a waiver for admission to a drug treatment center.

During the withdrawal period, Susan cursed her folks and the detestable place where she was locked up. But, after a while, she wrote a letter containing the first signs of a new day. "Dear Dad and Mother," it read.

> . . . I'm crying for the first time in many months, not because I'm hurt or angry, but because I'm happy. I know that I'm where I need to be and you all are doing this for me . . .
>
> Love and thanks,
> Susan

During her treatment, a concerned Christian instructor took special interest in Susan, including praying for her. On Susan's next to the last day at the center, this lady asked if she would want to give her life to Jesus Christ. Susan repented of her sins and asked Christ to come into her life. Jimmy described the result: "Susan walked out of the center that day in 1978 with the chemical balance of her system corrected and with a new life empowered by the Spirit of Christ."

Susan puts the climax on this family experience. "I started

experimenting with drugs because I didn't like myself or anything around me. Drugs gave me a good feeling, and everything looked better. The trouble was that my body built up tolerance and I had to take more and more drugs to keep up my high. This led me to heroin addiction. It made me hate the world, and my thinking became confused. But I didn't care.

"Daddy told you how I got into the drug treatment hospital. It was terrible, at first. They didn't give drugs to compensate for those I was taking. Instead, they quickly detoxified me of all the medication I was on. They took me in to clean me up. It was agonizing. It made me numb, with no emotions. I couldn't even cry. It gave me tremors and caused me to stutter. I couldn't sleep and was hallucinating. I tried to escape, but they caught me.

"After nearly three months, I began to feel better. They taught me skills. After about five months, they made plans to let me out. By then, I wanted to stay. The center had become my security. Going back into the world scared me. Thinking regular people would reject me, I was afraid of being with them. It made me cry just to think about it.

"The day before leaving, I was alone, crying on a bench on the campus. Another patient stopped to talk. She told me that she had accepted Jesus. I wanted the joy she had, so I decided to go and see my office occupation instructor one last time. We had become close friends. I knew she was a Christian. She asked if I would like for Jesus to come into my life because he could help me. I said, 'Yes, I would.' With another Christian instructor, we prayed. Right away I felt better.

"Then I wasn't afraid of going back home. I found that my family loved me. This made me feel good about myself. A weekly prayer group of different ages and denominations asked me to join them. I found a good Christian friend, and now I know several Christians.

"I think the Lord has something special for me. After what I've been through, I think he is going to use me in some particular way to help others. And, I'm ready. God is so good to me, and I'm so happy. I want others to know how Jesus can help them, like he helps me."

There is so much more to add, Jimmy Stallings says, but he concludes with this thought: "Being born again means more than receiving the crown of life hereafter, true as that is." That is the reward referred to by the apostle James: "For once his testing is complete he will receive the crown of life which the Lord has promised to all who love him" (1:12*b,* Phillips).

"Louise, Susan—our whole family knows firsthand that this also means receiving the winner's crown in this life," Jimmy adds.

Dad's Dream

Bertha Mabry—wife, mother, teacher, community leader at Marietta, Georgia—picks up Jimmy's thought. "I agree with Jimmy that every committed Christian is destined to win." She acknowledges that Christians, like anyone else, have problems, but quickly adds, "Problems faced with Christ become the basis of personal growth and progress. He helps us make something beautiful out of our difficulties, no matter what they are, if we trust him and let him work through us."

People who know Bertha and her husband, Hagood, say that Bertha is qualified to make such a statement. Particularly, they mention the Mabrys' bitter disappointments and crushing loads, along with the honors and community respect that have come their way.

As Bertha and Hagood were married and started their family, he dreamt of a son in big league basketball. When their third child, a son, arrived, Hagood quickly sized him up as the one. Sanford was husky, long and lanky. Dad's eyes sparkled.

As Sanford grew, the parents began to wonder. His responses did not seem on a par with those of other children the same age. When Sanford was eight months old, Bertha became seriously concerned, although doctors had not yet diagnosed him as being retarded. But retardation rapidly became apparent.

The blow came when Sanford was fourteen months old. The doctor, a specialist, advised, "He'll never walk or talk. My recommendation is to put him away."

"By God's leading," Bertha explains, "I was ready for the bitter advice. That morning before going to see the doctor, I felt very heavy. Even with prayer, the heaviness was hard to shake, but I kept on praying. Looking up from our porch, I saw Kennesaw mountain, and the scripture came to me, 'I lift up my eyes to the hills. From whence does my help come? My help comes from the Lord, who made heaven and earth' (Psalm 121:1-2).

"My faith began to feel restored. While driving to Atlanta, I found myself joyfully singing the words to Fosdick's hymn 'God of Grace and God of Glory.'

"So," says Bertha, "when the doctor gave her prognosis, it didn't phase me. By faith, I knew there was a better answer."

"Did you ever feel resentful?" I queried.

"Not really," she answered, "though I almost do when I think of the doctor's advice to put him away. My faith kept telling me that something good could come out of the problem. That sustained me. It took a long time. Today, with San at thirty, it's easy to see."

Bertha then recalled the excitement of seeing him take his first step at two and put together his first sentence at five. For three years or more, they had patiently helped him form words, which came slowly. But even one, whenever it came, was encouraging. Continuous prompting to put words together to make a sentence seemed fruitless.

Spurred by a Sentence

One night Bertha was putting San to bed, after her usual private time of quiet talking with him and evening prayer.

She could see something was on his mind. Then came his first sentence, "Mama, I love you."

"That," says Bertha, "was the answer to our faith and the reward for the extra patience and time it took to coax and train him to do things. We had been encouraging and helping him just like we did our other two children. But it took longer—so much longer."

That one sentence, spoken in 1956, was an anchor experience in the lives of the Mabrys. It gave them new hope and spurred their efforts to even more intensive promotion of his abilities.

Out of it came the almost impossible search for a school; the organization of a chapter of the Association for Retarded Children (ARC, now known as the Association for Retarded Citizens) in Cobb County; finding a special education teacher, then teachers; building a special, private school for the mentally retarded (MR).

The Mabrys' is a long, eventful story. Much centers around Bertha's divine call for teaching MRs and Hagood's leadership through the ARC. And uppermost, it includes the support of hard-working parents and friends to raise funds for the new school and for many other things to get the program for MRs underway.

"There was only one special education class in all of Cobb County," Bertha recalls. "With twenty-two children enrolled, it was crowded. Their acceptance of San was a miraculous answer to our prayers. Later, through the ARC, we hunted far and wide to get another special ed teacher. We prayed for that person. Nothing happened. No answer.

"During the search, I attended a revival in our church. At one of the services, I rededicated my life to the Lord. Kneeling at the altar, the word came clearly to me that I was the one to fill the teaching position for special education.

"For nine years I had been out of teaching and had only a three-year college teaching certificate. Compared with my position at Lockheed, it meant a 50 percent cut in salary. And there would be the cost for more schooling. I had no peace until I went to the school board and offered my services. It was my step forward in faith. I couldn't understand it, but I believed it.

"Subject to my agreeing to go back to school for ten summers to get special, advanced training, they immediately accepted and started me teaching special education. At thirty-eight, it was a new career."

Memories of the Miraculous

Fondly remembering firsthand the trials and errors of starting the various new programs in special ed, the Mabrys now see a graded system of training that takes the retarded all the way through the Cobb County High School, including a high school certificate.

With special satisfaction, they see the part San plays in their church—loving people, welcoming them, being concerned when someone is missing. They see his full-time employment, the happiness and zest with which he handles his responsibilities.

In 1978 the Cobb County school system was looking for candidates for their Teacher-of-the-Year award. Someone on the committee remembered the day Bertha volunteered to take on the job nobody else would take. Another person pointed out that the Cobb County school system is now one of the national leaders in special education, with programs for both trainable (TMR) and educable mentally retarded (EMR). A third observed that Cobb schools have trained special education student teachers from Auburn University, West Georgia, Georgia State, and the University of Georgia. Then someone spoke up about Bertha's dedication and about the part she played in the development of this now-famous program. Enthusiastically, the committee focused on Bertha Mabry. Out of almost three thousand teachers, she became Cobb County's 1978 Teacher-of-the-Year.

The state also recognized her accomplishments. For the

first time in Georgia history, a special education teacher, Bertha, became one of the top four Teachers-of-the-Year.

Bertha and Hagood frequently participate in Lay Witness Missions. Being spotlighted in one of these, Bertha said, in response to the honors she was receiving, "It's not I. Without my rebirth experience, it would never have been. It's Christ working through me. I just thank God that he called me, and by his grace, I responded. My experience is like Paul's as he writes, 'Glory be to him whose power, working in us, can do infinitely more than we can ask or imagine' (Ephesians 3:20, JB)."

As she describes how well Sanford is functioning today, Bertha concludes, "That's the boy the doctor said, 'Put away,' but the Lord said, 'I'll help you.'"

Hagood added a postcript for living: "I had one game in mind. The Lord showed us the possibilities of another. It's a lot more fun being a winner in the Lord's game than in mine."

Points to Ponder

* Christians, as well as non-Christians, have troubles in life. "'For he gives his sunlight to both the evil and the good, and sends rain on the just and on the unjust too'" (Matthew 5:45*b*, LB).
* Born-again Christians have a power through Christ for successful living that the noncommitted do not have.
* With a personal faith in Christ, tragedies can be turned into triumphs.
* We win by listening to God for his direction and by giving our abilities to him to use in working out his answers.
* With Christ, the tougher the battle, the greater the victory.
* Some struggles take longer than others to win.
* Christ's own words give us cheer for our challenges when he says, "'Here on earth you will have many trials and sorrows; but cheer up, for I have overcome the world'" (John 16:33*b*, LB).

CHAPTER 14

I Give In—and Win

*Though he slay me, yet will I trust in him. (Job 13:15*a, *KJV)*

I stopped by Estelle's office before leaving to put on an Imperial Homes sales meeting at Hartsville, South Carolina. She spoke a parting encouragement and then added, almost fearfully, "Did you see what happened to our schedule for next week? Four cancellations, leaving only one home for production." Estelle was the treasurer and responsible for cash flow.

How well I knew what had happened. We needed a house a day to break even. So we would suffer heavy losses, a sharp blow on cash flow.

The foul market mood had been threatening us for several months. The effect on our business had been a gradual slowdown, turning operations from profit to loss. We had been fighting hard to head off the inevitable, resulting from annualized housing starts plummeting from 2,400,000 to 1,400,000 in the past twelve months. This put us on our knees.

Out of our prayers had come affirmative action for turning slow sales to optimistic opportunity. The program became known as Imperial's Good News Sales Plan.

Plans and Prayers

To review and present the possibilities of this timely sales approach was the purpose of my Hartsville trip. There we had a star example. We were bringing in salespeople to show them how it could be done.

But now the abrupt Monday morning cancellations seriously affected our nerve and optimism for picking up a market when it was falling rapidly.

As I turned to go, Estelle virtually whispered, "Think we can hold out? Can we make it?"

Realizing I was behind schedule and having no assuring answer, my quick, nonetheless serious, response was, "Let's be in prayer. I'll call you early tomorrow morning to check out our answers."

Between stops en route to Aiken, South Carolina, for the night, my prayers were very pointed. *Lord, what do you want us to do, stay open or close up?*

While praying, I thought of our loyal employees. Profit-sharing had already been cut out. There were also the investments by our limited and select group of stockholders, relatives, and close friends. Then, too, we had developed an excellent group of suppliers. Our bills were piling up. Right now, we probably could close up and pay off everybody. How much longer would the bad market last? Could we really make an impact and go against the trend? Maybe this week at Hartsville would tell us whether we were dreaming or doing.

That night, there was no definite answer to my prayers. Maybe an answer will come while sleeping, I thought, and went to sleep praying.

In Estelle's Bible her note marked March 26, 1974, written early in the morning before I called, reminds us to this day of the word she passed to me.

> May he grant you your heart's desire,
>   and fulfill all your plans!
> May we shout for joy over your victory,
>   and in the name of our God set up our banners!
>
> (Psalm 20:4-5*a*)

Before calling Estelle, a word had also come to me. It, too, was powerful and propelling. "'Call upon me in the day of trouble; I will deliver you, and you shall glorify me'" (Psalm 50:15*b*).

Despite layoffs at the plant, much cash being lost, and housing starts still tumbling, I faced the day with renewed hope and faith. There were no visibly favorable signs, but those two positive words of Scripture caused me to believe better times were coming. This experience gave me a clear understanding of the Scripture's definition of faith: "What is faith? It is the confident assurance that something we want is going to happen. It is the certainty that what we hope for is waiting for us, even though we cannot see it up ahead" (Hebrews 11:1, LB).

The Hartsville trip gave me a lift. Betty Grainger's dramatically successful sales record was based on finding people who could qualify financially, graphically showing them how they could be approved for a new-home loan, and imparting to them courage to act despite the economic environment of fear and paralysis. She, too, prayed for understanding of every prospect's needs and for wisdom to give the right answers.

Betty's fantastic results—something like twenty sales in thirty days—were refreshing and revitalizing. She was the answer to our prayer for God to show us the way out of the morass of the market.

The Good News approach caught on. A number of Imperial builders and their salespeople picked up the idea. Despite a continuing market disintegration, finally plunging to below 1,000,000 starts, Imperial shipments gradually picked up. We cut overhead. We reduced our break-even. Although cash reserves had been seriously impaired, we were able to keep going. Many of our competitors closed up.

Coping with Pressures

We battled on. Fervent prayer gave us marketing strategies that attracted industry attention. Our sales meetings were well attended. National trade publications featured our strategies under such headlines as More in '74, Turn the Trend, Look Up, The Market-Buster Plan, and other creative, result-producing ideas. Several builders, joining our market-defying campaigns, literally turned the trend from depressed sales to increases and progress. Their success meant shipments to Imperial.

Although these programs kept Imperial alive, we were not able to rebuild our cash reserve. Our suppliers continued to cooperate, but only with a very restrictive line of credit. Two or three threatened suits but backed down when they were convinced of Imperial's efforts and determination to pull out of difficulties. Even so, too often Estelle had to start the day with a kind of desperation prayer: *Lord, I don't see any source of cash to meet today's bills. I can't handle it. I'm yours, you'll just have to take over.*

It amazes us as we recall the ways in which her prayers were answered—checks coming in earlier than expected, delayed billings with discount, account adjustments, unexpected rush orders, and many other ways. As a last resort, not too often, I would get on the phone and plead for consideration.

As time went on, the pressures became heavier and heavier. The only thing that kept us going was faith that God was with us and that somehow he was going to see us through, even deliver us.

Then something or someone planted the idea of bankruptcy in my mind. I recoiled. Words heard several years earlier from a friend came back. He said, "As long as there are crumbs on my table, I'll never file bankruptcy."

The very idea of bankruptcy was repugnant to me. It was the worst thing a person could do. It meant giving up faith, honor, and the integrity of our word, which we had spent a lifetime developing. It was like being a turncoat on those who trust and love you. It was unthinkable.

As we faced threatened suits, two unexpected facts emerged: Bankruptcy protects all creditors with a fair share of remaining assets, and an irate creditor could cause involuntary bankruptcy.

Facing these realities and my abhorrence of bankruptcy, I began to wonder, *What would I do?* I couldn't face it. To where could I escape? another state, overseas? where?

Again, it was to my knees. *How could this destructive possibility be handled in a Christian way?*

Out of this desperate cry came three ideas: merge, bring in new management and additional capital, or sell out. Our board approved my exploring these options.

Some good companies were ready to talk merger. One went so far as to outline plans for dividing responsibilities of the executive staffs, plans that were presented to the boards for approval. Imperial directors approved, but despite the carefully designed, progressive plans, the other board did not approve.

New Hope

The possibility of bringing in new management and additional capital gave us new hope. A longtime friend, Bill Brown, turned out to be our best prospect. Our friendship had started several years previously when we brought him in as advertising manager of Kingsberry Homes. He did an outstanding job and went on to other responsibilities in the industry. He made a name for himself as a brilliant plant operator. As we progressed, we kept in touch, appreciating each other's efforts and work.

We discovered that Bill was also interested in taking on ownership responsibilities. Imperial's board worked out a plan whereby he could pick up a substantial holding in the company. But Bill wasn't quite ready to make the move. The door was left open for later consideration. His proposition was the brightest thing we could see for the future.

The struggle for survival continued. Some days there would be a glimmer of light. Then, as though a black curtain closed, we would be in total darkness, not knowing which way to turn. Strangely, looking back, we reduced our accounts payable. Our most valuable personnel loyally fought the battle with Estelle and me and our investors. We strengthened our position with creditors by the entire plant, except Estelle and me, taking a 60 percent paycheck. We drew out no salary.

By the grace and wisdom of God, we pulled through a day at a time. The squeeze slowly, relentlessly became more and more agonizing. By this time our fight for survival had been going on for thirty-four months.

Despair and Uncertainty

Thursday, January 6, 1977, 6:30 A.M., I went to our United Methodist Men's prayer and fellowship breakfast at Al and Belle Blanton's home. Leaving about ten minutes early, I walked out with Merrill Arnold, a close friend. Coming to my car first, we chatted for a moment. Then Merrill asked in a confidential tone, "How are things working out, Gus?"

"Slow," I responded.

Then I broke, feeling the pressure. Embarrassingly, I cried. The tears showed the helplessness of my feelings. Merrill graciously gave me encouragement, and we both went on.

But the tears had started, and I couldn't stop them. My crying turned into uncontrolled sobbing. The utter hopelessness of our situation came crushing down on me.

Instead of going to the office, I went home. There was no way to go, except prayer—specific prayer. My cry to God was, *Dear God, you see our desperation. We don't know what to do or where to turn. You've said, "Call upon me in the day of trouble; I will deliver you." Lord, we're in trouble, deep trouble. We've been calling on you. We don't see delivery. Where are you? We believe that you led us into this business. We believe that you do not want us to be a dishonor to you. We know we've made mistakes. We believe you forgive us and will help us to do better. Lord, we need answers. Tell us what to do—today. We're listening and waiting. Thank you Lord. We believe, even now, you're helping us. Amen.*

The first word was to call Estelle to come home, asking her to pray as she came. Waiting, I received two names—Bill Brown and Sam Teague.

Exploring what could be done when everything seemed impossible, Estelle's only idea was to check again with Bill to see if his timetable could be pushed up. I had not told her of the names that came to me, so we regarded this as definite confirmation of step one.

Bill's response was, "Gus, you called at just the right time. I'm more disillusioned than ever with my present situation."

Sam Teague, our banking friend, recommended, "You should contact the Small Business Administration. As a recent board member, I know they have lots of money and are pushing to get it out." Then he added, "Gus, we all go through these things. The Lord is with you. You're going to have an answer. It will work out."

The good news of Bill's response channeled all our efforts in his direction. We got together. A date for his joining Imperial was set for February 1977 after he had fulfilled his responsibilities for earning the sizable bonus he had coming.

As we waited, another company—one of the biggest home manufacturers, a multimillion-dollar company visualizing sales of a billion dollars—got on Bill's trail, determined to get him. They gave roses to his wife, Merle, and to the two of them a luxurious trip and VIP entertaining, climaxed by a fabulous financial offer. Bill kept us informed and assured us that his commitment was with Imperial.

We held on. The uncertainty was a nightmare. Every day we had to work out ways to pay bills; negotiate with suppliers to get materials; fight FHA for sales approvals, spending two to four months per case, even longer; reassure our employees, although all we had to offer was hope and partial income; figure how much longer Estelle and I could hold out without salaries, expecting that any moment an impatient supplier would lose faith in us and file suit, which would be the end.

Give-It-Up Praying

On January 27, 1977, there was another "wrestling with the Lord." I wrote down the following prayer of commitment that emerged. I call it my Give-It-Up prayer. Until this encounter with the Lord, I was afraid of this kind of praying.

Good morning, My Lord—

Thank you for speaking to me yesterday morning, as I was traveling to Atlanta, about closing or not closing IH.

Thank you, dear Lord.

We've prayed.

Friends have prayed.

We've given money as seed faith.

We've trusted, believed, and served you.

We've praised you in our difficulties.

We acknowledge our failures but believe that with you we can rise above them. Forgive us. We thank you that you do.

Now, help me, Lord, to recall and write down our conversation of yesterday.

1. My opening claim: Within our human limitations, we've done everything we know or can think of at this time. Then, your prompting: You have shown us many ways to keep Imperial going. Next, my commitment: We'll continue as long as you show us a way, even a day at a time.

2. My acknowledgment: We believe that IH is a trust from you, and as such, you don't want us to run away from responsibilities to owners, suppliers, and employees.

3. With our own power, we haven't been able to save IH. We've come to trust you for saving it, so we're in your hands.

4. We believe in you—that you're almighty and all powerful.

5. Thank you for your reminder: It's within your power to close us down or to deliver us, even to get us out of this trouble.

6. My admission to you: We're at your mercy and at your call. Your will be done.

7. Another commitment to you: If Imperial closes down, it's because you close us down.

8. Your reassurance: This isn't blaming you, but our believing you know best and see things we don't see—perhaps even "great and mighty things."

9. My understanding: So if you deliver us, we know it's your will—only you can do it. I give up. It's beyond me. If you will, we would be victors instead of victims. That's what we would like.

10. My bold conclusion: Lord, even if you bankrupt us, I'm ready to say, like Job, "Though he slay me, yet will I trust in him." Yes, finally, I am able to say: If you're with me, I can face bankruptcy right here in Griffin, if necessary. God help me.

Dear God, I'm amazed at this conversation. We could have it only through the power and love of your son, Jesus. Thank you. Amen.

Some people might criticize me as copping out and not fully using my God-given gifts and abilities. My reply would be that after all the excruciating effort, we had become weaker and weaker. I felt helpless and had only one answer—God.

The Bible, the foundation of my faith, told me to turn my worries over to him. In that conversational struggle, words strongly came through to me, such as, "Come to me, all of you who are tired from carrying heavy loads, and I will give you rest" (Matthew 11:28, GNB); "'What is impossible for man is possible for God'" (Luke 18:27*b*, GNB); and "Trust in the Lord with all thine heart; and lean not unto thine own understanding. In all thy ways acknowledge him, and he shall direct thy paths" (Proverbs 3:5-6, KJV).

So my giving up was conditional—to God's will for me.

Personally developed plans hadn't worked. The bottom line of my faith challenged me. Did I really believe or not? If so, the next and only step was to put it on God. So I talked to him and accepted his leading—whatever! This was my commitment.

A day or two later, Bill called to say he had an appointment set up with a new investor he planned to bring into the company. On February 15, 1977, we met. There were all the appearances of our coming together. We were to hear in two or three days.

The days came and went, and no word. Then they called, saying it would take another week. Time, inexorably, was running out—too fast.

Overture

While waiting for the investor's word, Bill had a most unusual communication from the company so determined to get him into their camp. He phoned me. "Gus," he started out, "I've had a call I don't know how to handle. From the Far East the chairman of the board called, saying, 'Tell Brown that whatever his obligation is to that Georgia company, we will take it over. We want to get into the Sunbelt market. Will they talk with us?'"

Knowing the tremendous offer they were making Bill, I replied, "Bill, go ahead, take the job, and certainly we'd be interested in seeing what we could work out with them."

Bill took the job, and on February 22, we met with his new company. Their interest was genuine. We were to meet again soon.

Days went by, and no word. My follow-up call, trying to get the meeting arranged before it was too late, was responded to with the statement, "Our key people are tied up in meetings and under pressures of booming business. We're still interested. We'll call you as soon as we can."

That answer made each day bleaker than the day before. Could it be that God was going to close us down after all? I hung on to Job's affirmation. It gave me courage, but on Tuesday, March 2, I had to say to Estelle, "If something doesn't happen before Monday, it looks like bankruptcy. Some creditors won't stand by any longer."

Wednesday, our daughter Gwen stopped by. As we told her of the pending circumstances, I broke. I could not stand to think of the disgrace this would bring to our children. Responding to my tears, she consoled, "Daddy, don't worry about it. We understand. We think just as much of you as if this hadn't happened. We know you and mother have done everything you could. Businesses do go broke. That's the risk of going into business. We love you just as much."

On Thursday or Friday our son Gerrit called from Mobile. He knew of our basic troubles but not of our imminent decision. He said, "I called to tell you I've been praying for you. Everything's going to be all right."

On Friday or Saturday came a note from Gwen's husband, Bob Hill, with the message, "Don't let your situation get you down. We're behind you. The trade respects you." He was in the building supply business, and we had several contacts in common.

Encouraged, we pulled ourselves together as I took off for Atlanta on Monday morning to see our attorney and initiate bankruptcy proceedings. Before leaving, I ran into our pastor, Lamar Cherry. He confidentially said, "Dolly and I prayed for your success this morning." Al and Belle Blanton and Merrill and Jane Arnold had told us virtually the same thing over the weekend.

On the way to Atlanta, Brother Lamar's words came back to me. Then I thought about all the others who were praying, along with the encouragement and support from Gwen, Bob, and Gerrit. The thought persisted in my mind, *There must be some way . . .*

At that moment, I remembered Teague's words, "You should talk with the Small Business Administration."

Having our financial statements with me, I went to SBA instead of our attorney. After analyzing the statements and asking questions about our experience, the reviewing officer reported, "This looks possible. I believe we can work out something. Fill out this application, and let's see what we can do."

That put a hold on bankruptcy. Creditors were hoping this would be their answer.

The same afternoon Estelle called to say that Bill Brown and other representatives of his new company wanted to come down and meet with us on March 17.

Negotiations proceeded smoothly. The proposals looked good to our board. On August 30, 1977, the deal was closed, and Imperial became the southern facility of one of the housing giants in the industry.

Imperial Flag-raising

Even before the deal was closed, Estelle, reminded by the March notation in her Bible, gave an Imperial flag-raising party. We invited several who had prayed so fervently with us. We remembered "May he grant you your heart's desire . . ."

In the name of our God, we won!

One obligation remained—the morning we compared God's directions to us, the Lord's word to me was "'You shall glorify me.'"

Our flag-raising party was one effort to glorify him by sharing with others his miraculous deliverance of Imperial Homes.

After the party the thought came,

Isn't glorifying him what he has wanted me to do ever since he called me? At least that is my prayer.

Thank you, Lord, for the sacred, exciting, supportive call to being a layman. It gives such dynamic purpose and power for living. To you be the glory. Amen.

Points to Ponder

* For the Christian, when there seems no way to turn, there is God.

* Winning for God requires struggle, sometimes more than winning for self.
* God offers supernatural power to fight battles for him.
* If God is in the conflict, there can be peace in the battle.
* Giving up to God means coming up with answers.
* God's ways are often not our ways.
* Christians have no insurance against bad weather, tough times, and life's unpredictability.
* God calls us to take on heavy responsibilities and offers help when loads would get us down.

APPENDIX

Discovering a New or Enlarged Call

A Prayer

My dear Lord, Jesus Christ,

I believe you. I want to serve you—to be useful to you—and to have the motivating confidence that I am fulfilling your purpose for my life. And, Lord, you know that, in the depths of my heart, there is the urge to glorify you.

Where You Are

(Cross out the paragraph below that does not apply to your life.)

1. I haven't fully discovered your purpose for me. It is my prayer that you will reveal it. Help me to have an open heart and an open mind so I can clearly see the special thing you have for me to do.
2. You have blessed me by speaking about your purpose for my life. I don't understand the greatness and wonder of it all or where it might lead. Help me to give myself more completely to the tremendous experience of being your person where you need me. Help me to be alert to the unfolding of exciting new opportunities for serving you.

__________ ____________________

Date Name

Possible Next Steps

Start now—these are the miracle words of God's great call for your life.

Very possibly, he has already spoken to you in some special, personal way. If so, jump up and start right away, as Matthew did when he was called.

If you need more definitive direction, a clearer word from the Lord, try one of the following.

1. **Be a brave Christian.** Order the booklet *The John Wesley Great Experiment* and its companion piece, *A Life That Really Matters.* The experiment is to see what happens when you practice five disciplines of Christian living for thirty days. The lives of thousands of people around the world have taken on new meaning and purpose while performing this exercise. You may order it from the Board of Discipleship, P. O. Box 840, Nashville, Tennessee 37202. Currently, around $3.00 for the set.

2. **Latch on to the power of prayer.** *The Workbook of Living Prayer* will raise the level of your prayer power. Out of it will come insights that will inspire you to new heights of living and service. Order it through Abingdon, P. O. Box 801, Nashville, Tennessee 37202. Currently, $3.95.

3. **Be a volunteer in mission—where you are.** Like Red Bond, go to your pastor or to one of the officials of your church and volunteer to do what needs to be done. Or, find something that no one is doing. Done in the name of Christ and because of your love for him, this will be the first step in a life of unfolding peace, purpose, and power.

NOTES

Preview

1. Elton Trueblood, *The Common Ventures of Life: Marriage, Birth, Work and Death* (New York: Harper & Row, 1949), p. 86.

Chapter 1.

1. Venture in Discipleship resources are available through Discipleship Resources, P.O. Box 840, Nashville, Tennessee 37202. Discipleship resources catalogs are also available at this address.

Chapter 2.

1. Traditional.
2. Carl F. H. Henry, "Evangelicals: Out of the Closet but Going Nowhere?" *Christianity Today,* January 4, 1980, p. 20.
3. Materials available through Discipleship Resources.
4. G. Ross Freeman, "Guard the Treasure" (Address made at Epworth by the Sea, March 17, 1979).
5. Win Arn, "Mass Evangelism the Bottom Line," *Church Growth: America,* January–February 1978, p. 7.

Chapter 3.

1. Harold Rogers, *Harry Denman: A Biography* (Nashville: The Upper Room, 1977), pp. 57-58.
2. William Cowper, "Light Shining Out of Darkness."

Chapter 4.

1. Resources available through Discipleship Resources.
2. Walk Thru the Bible Ministries, P.O. Box 720653, Atlanta, Georgia 30328.

Experience II

1. Lloyd John Ogilvie, *When God First Thought of You: The Full Measure of Love as Found in 1, 2, 3 John* (Waco, Tex.: Word Books, 1978), p. 183.

Chapter 5.

1. Ogilvie, *When God First Thought of You,* p. 156.
2. Ed Robb, "How Can I Know God's Will?" *Challenge,* Spring 1980, p. 8. The incident is related in J. B. Phillips' *The Ring of Truth* (reprint ed., Wheaton, Ill.: Harold Shaw Publishers, 1977).
3. Leslie D. Weatherhead, *The Will of God* (Nashville: Abingdon, 1978), pp. 47-51.
4. Ibid., p. 46.
5. *The Upper Room Daily Devotional Guide,* March–April, 1980, p. 33.
6. Weatherhead, *The Will of God,* p. 47.

Chapter 6.

1. Ogilvie, *When God First Thought of You,* pp. 139-40.
2. Wm H. Danforth, *I Dare You* (St. Louis: The Danforth Foundation, 1978), p. 7.

Chapter 8.

1. *D. W. Brooks—A Great Georgian,* film (Athens, Ga.: University of Georgia Extension Service).

Chapter 9.

1. Trueblood, *The Common Ventures of Life,* p. 87.
2. Resources available through Discipleship Resources.

Chapter 10.

1. *North Myrtle Beach Times* (S.C.), August 11, 1977, p. 7.
2. *Laymen Committed to Expanding Lay Witnessing* (Griffin, Ga.: Georgia Laity Board of Renewal, 1978).
3. Kenneth Chafin (Address made at Robert H. Schuller Institute for Successful Church Leadership, tape, Garden Grove, Calif.: Robert H. Schuller, January 1981).

Chapter 11.

1. Lloyd Ogilvie, *Life Without Limits* (Waco, Tex.: Word Books, 1975), pp.195-96.

Chapter 12.

1. Wallace E. Johnson, *Together We Build: The Life and Faith of Wallace E. Johnson* (New York: Hawthorn Books, 1973 and 1978), p. 8.
2. Wallace E. Johnson, *Guideposts,* April 1967, p. 13.
3. Johnson, *Together We Build,* pp. 62-63.
4. Ibid., p. 99.
5. Ibid., pp. 181-82.
6. Ibid., pp. 183-84.
7. Ibid., pp. 178-79.

Chapter 13.

1. The toll-free number is 1-800-251-2468.